NATIONAL BILINGUALISM IN PARAGUAY

JANUA LINGUARUM

STUDIA MEMORIAE
NICOLAI VAN WIJK DEDICATA

edenda curat

C. H. VAN SCHOONEVELD
INDIANA UNIVERSITY

SERIES PRACTICA
60

1968
MOUTON
THE HAGUE · PARIS

NATIONAL BILINGUALISM IN PARAGUAY

by

JOAN RUBIN

THE GEORGE WASHINGTON UNIVERSITY

1968

MOUTON

THE HAGUE · PARIS

ACKNOWLEDGMENTS

It is impossible to realize the importance of the persons mentioned in the acknowledgments of a book until you yourself write one. In a sense, it is impossible to express gratitude for all the time, encouragement, and helpful suggestions I have received from professors, informants, colleagues, friends, and family. Yet, the mention of their names at the beginning is some small token of thanks.

The original formulation of a research problem derives from classes and discussions which I had with Paul Garvin at the University of Michigan. The field research and dissertation writing were supervised by Floyd G. Lounsbury and I am deeply appreciative of his help and criticism.

The field study and dissertation writing were made possible through grant number MF-11,528 from the National Institutes of Mental Health, United States Public Health Service. The 1965 study was subsidized by grants from the National Science Foundation and the Wenner-Gren Foundation for Anthropological Research.

The help I got from Paraguayan friends deserves special mention. I continually and consistently got full support, introductions to the community, and many explanations from my assistant Tadeo Gonzalez, my "godmother" Georgina Correa, and my Itapuami hosts, Manuel and Lidia Galeano. My Asunción friend, Lorenzo Livieres, was always available to help orient me to Asunción. The noted Paraguayan historian, Efraím Cardozo, whom I met in 1965, generously made available his own notes on Paraguayan bilingualism, many of which are extremely hard to locate in the numerous historical documents.

I am indebted for comments and criticism on the dissertation to Ruth Krulfeld, A. Richard Diebold, Richard Jolly, Janet Duckett, and Bruce Trigger. Subsequent discussions about the dissertation results with Fred Adelman and Stephen Boggs helped clarify some of the theoretical material. Thanks for editorial comments on the dissertation are due Bernarda Erwin and my sister, Louise Goldstein; thanks for editorial comments on the book are due June Helm and F. T. Cloak, Jr.

Finally, three persons helped with typing, tabulating, proofing, and in general lending a hand when there was some "busy work" to be done. I consider it an honor to have had such help from my mother, Ann Rubin, and my friends, Jean Pierre Poullier and Harold Hollingsworth. This book would not have been possible without the excellent assistance of all these people and I am very pleased to acknowledge their contributions.

PREFACE

This book is a study of one bilingual area within the very bilingual country, Paraguay. The title implies that the patterns herein described for this one area obtain throughout the country. I feel that this is essentially an accurate picture because of the cultural homogeneity by which Paraguay can be characterized. Except for a few areas where there is a large immigrant population and those areas where there are scattered groups of isolated Indians, there is an overall structural regularity to Paraguayan culture.

My purpose in this study is to describe and analyze the cultural, political, and social factors patterning individual behavior related to the two major languages of Paraguay — Spanish and Guarani. I examine extensively four interdependent factors — attitudes, stability, usage, and acquisition and proficiency — which appear to reflect the social, cultural, and political structure of the area. I have tried to indicate how these characteristics are dependent upon the history of contact between the aboriginal Paraguayan population and the Spanish conquerors and upon the subsequent acculturation occasioned by this contact. A description of the present socio-economic setting of the area studied is given.

This study was originally presented as a doctoral dissertation to the Department of Anthropology of Yale University in 1963. The revised form herein presented includes additional references to recent literature on Paraguayan bilingualism, insights gained through study of more recent literature on componential analysis, and observations made during the past summer (June—August, 1965) when I returned to Paraguay to study indications of culture change in bilingual usage.

The impressions gained from this past summer lead me to suspect that Paraguay is slowly becoming more bilingual, moving from monolingual Guarani speakers to more bilinguals. However, I feel that bilingualism will remain a stable feature for a long time to come in Paraguay rather than serve as a transitional phase in a process leading toward monolingualism. (This latter phenomenon is the more prevalent one in a country like Peru). The reasons for the continuation of a stable bilingualism are expounded in this book but may be said to include such things as separation of language usage areas, lack of extended or extensive contact with Spanish speaking areas for most of the population and the positive association between Guarani and Paraguayan nationalism. Some of the changes which I observed in

1965 which led to the impression of increased bilingualism are: (1) The advent of cheap transistor radios has brought a limited amount of the urban culture to the countryside. Everyone now listens to the radio even though most of what is heard is music or sports. (2) The feeling seems to be increasing that it is better in formal rural situations to use Spanish if possible. Young men indicated that they addressed young girls at dances in Spanish to be polite. (3) There is an increase in the frequency of contact of the townsmen with Asunción which can be observed in the increased number of persons traveling daily to the capital. There is also an increase in the number of persons from the rural area studied, Itapuami, who travel both to Luque, the nearby town, and to Asunción. Such travel has been facilitated by the improvement in the road and a concomitant increase in bus travel.

The site of the major part of the study was a rural town, Luque, and a rural farming area near Luque, called Itapuami. In the rural area three major procedures were used to obtain data for comparative purposes: a complete house-to-house census of Itapuami and a random sample census of the town of Luque were taken; a linguistic questionnaire was given to one bilingual member of each household; and interviews were conducted and observations made at all of the schools in these two areas.

I spent a great deal of time visiting the schools and interviewing the teachers about their daily pedagogical problems and held group discussions with teachers about the problems which monolingual Guarani-speaking children present. I also interviewed and made friends with town leaders — social, religious, and political.

In addition to the objective schedules listed above, I also made a great many observations through the traditional anthropological technique of participant observation. Opportunities to do so were much more frequent and natural, however, in the smaller world of the rural area than in the more complex town.

Part of my time in Paraguay was spent in the capital, Asunción, interviewing poets, writers, government officials, students of the Guarani language, and other individuals interested in promoting the aboriginal language, Guarani. I also interviewed other educated persons and upper class persons to determine their attitudes towards the two languages. A large portion of my time in Asunción was spent trying to learn Guarani. This proved to be a difficult task. Since everyone in Asunción was, for all intents and purposes, bilingual, my knowledge of Spanish was a hindrance because it kept me from having to learn Guarani. It was only when I settled in the rural area that I acquired a relatively fluent command of Guarani. I also spent time in Asunción working at the Archives, at the Census Bureau, and at the Office of Education.

Comparative data with the area of Luque was available from two sources: the field study by the Services in Tobatí (Service, 1954b) and my own observations of the surrounding rural area of Luque and visits to the less central areas of the country: Concepción in the north, and Avaí and Itakyry in the east.

Among the difficulties I encountered in doing this field study were several problems often associated with research in a *large* community. There is the continual problem of establishing rapport in a community of some 11,000 persons. Such rapport is, of course, essential to the observation of natural speech. In my original study I found that it was relatively easy to do so in the rural area but relatively difficult to do in the town. Since a great deal of social interaction occurs in the home, one solution to the problem (which I thought of after returning home) would be to select several representative families in the town and try to live with each of them for a period long enough to pass the "politeness" barrier and get more "natural" data. Another problem which arose in the town is the difficulty with getting data on code-switching. This phenomenon only occurs in the most casual environment. A third problem which has not yet been solved is that of judging on objective grounds the linguistic competence of a speaker. This problem is heightened since there are always limitations of time and an ever-present crowd of helpful friends and relatives.

Insofar as I did not solve these problems in the field this study suffers. However, the study does offer a more detailed description and analysis of the sociolinguistics of a bilingual situation than is available for most areas.

The Paraguayan setting is an interesting one for sociolinguists because of the stability of its bilingual nature and because of the considerable complexity in the four factors studied (attitudes, usage, stability, and acquisition and proficiency), in spite of a fairly homogeneous community and the use of only two languages. Perhaps in helping to unravel here a relatively "simple" situation I have shed some light on the ways in which social, historical, and linguistic phenomena are interrelated and articulated.

JOAN RUBIN

University of North Carolina
Chapel Hill, North Carolina

March 23, 1966

TABLE OF CONTENTS

I. INTRODUCTION

Many areas of the world can be characterized by communication complexity which comes as a result of multilingualism. It is only in more recent years that social scientists have begun to examine and describe in detail the nature of this complexity. The focus of this book will be one such area of communication complexity, the bilingual nation, Paraguay. It is our intent to describe and analyze the social, political, and cultural factors patterning individual behavior related to the two major languages of Paraguay — Spanish and Guarani.

An understanding of the nature and functioning of bilingual communities is required for the resolution of a number of practical problems in national policy. Such understanding may also shed light on several theoretical problems in the study of culture contact and culture change. The practical problems posed by bilingualism — language planning and national development — in part have existed for many years and in part have been raised by the numerous postwar creations of new nations. In language planning, two basic problems often arise: (1) the need to bring the formal linguistic structure of one language to an accepted standard, and (2) the need to promote one language as the only acceptable medium in certain spheres, such as administration, education, and legislation. Both the creation of a state and the process of national development, in a multilingual community, require language planning. Effective language planning requires an understanding of social, ethnic, geographic, and political loyalties. In many countries decisions to promote one language above another have met with resistance when the language chosen was not one to which all groups owed their first loyalty.

The study of bilingualism may also contribute to understanding the process of culture change. Whenever two cultures with different languages have come into contact or whenever dialect divisions have arisen, when communication was continuous, some socio-linguistic adjustment has been made for the existing linguistic differences. The adjustment made depends upon the nature of the contact and the type of socio-economic communities which come into contact. The way in which this adjustment is made is partially reflected in the socio-linguistic behavior of bilinguals. An understanding of the reasons for becoming a bilingual may suggest directions in which the acculturation process is moving.

Although a considerable body of literature on bilingualism is available, our present knowledge of the interrelationship between socio-cultural systems and bilingualism is very limited. Only a few descriptive studies of actual bilingual communities exist (Diebold, 1961b; Haugen, 1953; and Weinreich, 1951, are among the most complete). The literature discussing theoretical problems in bilingualism is also limited, and in general suggests problems to be investigated rather than presents an integrated analytical framework (Weinreich, 1953; Haugen, 1956; Fishman, 1964). It would appear that more socio-linguistic studies are needed if a comprehensive theory is to be developed.

The present study is an attempt to help fill this need for actual field studies of bilingual communities. Our concern in this book will be to examine the Paraguayan bilingual community primarily from the socio-cultural point of view, both historically as well as socially. I hope that the analysis herein presented will not only contribute to a greater understanding of bilingual communities and more especially to an understanding of the unique Paraguayan situation, but that it will also provide some understanding of, and theoretical insights into, the general problems raised by bilingual phenomena.

In Paraguay, two languages, Spanish and Guarani, have coexisted for the past three hundred years in relative equilibrium. A high percentage (52%) of the community is said to be bilingual and almost the entire community (92%) can speak the aboriginal language, Guarani. Such an extended coexistence of two languages raises several questions:

(1) What historical factors explain the persistent importance of Guarani in Paraguay? In the rest of Latin America the aboriginal language has become secondary to Spanish, the language of the conquerors. Paraguay presents an exception: Guarani is still spoken by most Paraguayans and a high percentage of the population is bilingual.

(2) What factors, social, political, or economic, sustain this bilingual equilibrium? What factors may produce changes in the equilibrium?

(3) What attitudes do Paraguayans have toward each of their languages? To what extent is one language primary and the other secondary? Does one language have prestige and pride associated with it while the other is rejected or scorned? What do people think about the supposed positive attributes of each language?

(4) What social factors determine the linguistic usage of bilinguals? Are the areas of usage of each language mutually exclusive or is there a great deal of overlapping?

(5) Are both languages recognized by the State as official? If they are not, why not? If one is not official, is there any pressure for its recognition?

In order to answer these questions, I studied and then analyzed institutional and individual behavior toward both languages. The field study was primarily conducted in the subdivisons of the District of Luque in the Central Department. I intensively studied two representative areas within this Department: Luque, a town of approximately 11,000 inhabitants, and Itapuami, a rural community with approximately 1,300 inhabitants. In addition, some data on language usage was collected in the cities of Asunción and Concepción; data for the historical chapter was collected both in the National Archives and in government offices.

In addition to the development of an historical rationale for the persistence of Guarani, the analysis focuses on four aspects of extra-linguistic behavior: attitudes, usage, stability, and acquisition and proficiency. These four factors appear to be crucial in any study of the socio-linguistics of a bilingual community. The four are interdependent. They are also dependent upon the type of initial contact between communities involved, the subsequent equilibrium established, the cultural content of the communities, and the types of communities subsequently established.

In studying Paraguayan bilingualism as it relates to these four factors, I drew heavily on concepts already in the literature. Perhaps the area most clearly delineated was that of attitudes. Two classic papers were extremely suggestive: Garvin and Mathiot's paper "The Urbanization of the Guarani Language: A Problem in Language and Culture" (1960), and Ferguson's "Diglossia" (1959a), and of course, Weinreich's book *Languages in Contact* (1953) was an invaluable source.

A bilingual situation may be expected to produce different types of attitudes; some reflect the emotional value of a language for its speakers, others the value of a language from a social or group point of view, still others reflect its value from the point of view of formal attributes. Of those isolated in the literature, those which apply to Paraguay are: "language loyalty", pride, "prestige", "awareness of usage norms", and "awareness of linguistic norms".

The term "language loyalty" refers to "the name given to the desire of a speech community to retain its language and, if necessary, to defend it against foreign encroachment" (Weinreich, 1953, p. 99). Manifestations of this attitude can be seen in the way in which "people will rally themselves and their fellow speakers consciously and explicitly to resist changes in either the functions of their language (as a result of a language shift) or in the structure of vocabulary (as a consequence of interference)" (Weinreich, 1953, p. 99).[1]

Feelings of language loyalty are provoked when in a contact situation there is an attack on a language. Mother tongue speakers are said to have in their language a latent emotional involvement which is brought to the surface by attack. If, in the post-contact situation, a language is not in a dominant position, an attack may bring out feelings of superiority or inferiority. Feelings of inferiority may cause the speaker to praise the mother tongue while remaining basically unsure of its superiority (Weinreich, 1953).

[1] Both Barker, 1948, and Garvin and Mathiot, 1960, found the concept of language loyalty extremely important in understanding the bilingual community. Garvin and Mathiot said that language loyalty stemmed from the unifying and separatist function of a standard language. Barker spoke of language as a symbol of local patriotism, this being one of the two potential functions of a language in a bilingual situation (See note 4 following for second function).

Weinreich, 1953, also suggested that attitudes of language loyalty are not necessarily parallel with nationalistic aspirations. An ethnic group may defend its language even though to do so might be contrary to the goals of the nation. These expressions of loyalty may serve to separate rather than unite a linguistic group with the national community.

In Paraguay the term language loyalty characterizes a familiar attitude toward Guarani and not toward Spanish. Analysis shows that Guarani is the object of continual attack and defense and that this language is thought by many to be symbolic of Paraguayan nationalism.[2]

Another attitude toward language, pride, is important in understanding sociolinguistic behavior in a bilingual community.[3] A speaker may show his pride in his mother tongue by attributing to it special properties, real or alleged, and by pointing to its literary-cultural heritage. This heritage, its speakers may feel, gives their language greater significance than one which is only "spoken".

It is not always possible in a bilingual situation to predict which of the languages will evoke pride. The preferred language or the language of pride may vary from situation to situation. Nader, 1962, calls attention to the fact that prestige (which corresponds to my use of pride) is not necessarily related to "the affluent position of one group or another, or of one individual or another" (p. 45). Even though one may have a fairly rigidly structured society and associate one of the languages in a bilingual situation with a higher status group, all languages may have pride associated with them and the one singled out for special praise is not necessarily the one associated with the higher status group.

Support for the continued use of a favored language is often based on the claim that the language connects the community with its glorious past and/or with the world community. This pride in the superiority of a language may even serve as a block to communication. A monolingual speaker may prefer to hear a ceremonial function performed in a language he does not understand because of the supposed beauty of expression or sacredness of this language.

A separation between language loyalty and pride has been maintained here. In actual fact, there is an interrelation which makes it difficult to separate the two. Pride may exist without expression of language loyalty, whereas language loyalty cannot exist if there is no pride.

Both Spanish and Guarani are objects of pride in Paraguay. In discussing the Guarani language, speakers often suggest that they prefer it as a medium in which to speak of love, to tell jokes, and to write poetry. Some speakers claim that Guarani

---

[2]   Garvin and Mathiot, 1960, suggested in their paper that language loyalty was a prominent attitude in Paraguay. My analysis substantiated this suggestion through actual field study and also pointed to the lack of a need for such an attitude toward Spanish.

[3]   This term is used by Garvin and Mathiot, 1960. Ferguson, 1959a, also listed this attitude (he called it "prestige") as important in understanding the nature of bilingual communities. He mentioned the importance of a literary-cultural heritage for diglossia. In other bilingual situations emphasis on this heritage may be taken as a rationalization for attitudes of pride.

permits the expression of certain concepts which are difficult to express with precision in Spanish. While the literary heritage of Guarani is relatively weak, attempts are being made to strengthen it. On the other hand, Spanish is not usually the object of pride but those who prefer to speak Spanish suggest it is a more useful language because it serves as a medium of wider communication and because it does have an important literary heritage.

Another attitude frequently described as important in bilingual communities is "prestige". The term has been used indiscriminately for other concepts often connected with prestige.[4] Weinreich, 1953, proposed the limitation of the term to "the value of a language in social advance" (p. 79).[5] "Social advance" means that knowledge of a language will enable the speaker to improve his social status. In some situations bilingual knowledge has only the "practical" function of communication. In others, it has certain useful "social" functions. Haugen, 1956, isolated two functions of language: (1) communication and (2) social identification.[6] Social identification may be with a "higher" or "better" social group. "Better" need not always mean higher social status; some individuals may prefer to identify with a group which is at the lower end of the social scale. If this is true, then desires for social identification are not necessarily associated with attitudes of prestige.

Another attitude which may be associated with extra-linguistic behavior in a bilingual community is an awareness of usage norms. That is, in certain situations, correct usage may be so narrowly formulated that misusage is noticed. Goodenough, 1961, suggested that regular patterns of usage behavior may be manipulated by speakers to achieve certain effects. The result of such "misuse" may be shock, insult, intimacy, or humor. A deviation may be recognized only when there is a set of patterns accepted as appropriate by most participants.

Finally, an attitude labeled "awareness of linguistic norms"[7] is commonly found in those bilingual situations where one of the languages is the object of a standardization process. In Paraguay, as Garvin and Mathiot, 1960, suggested, there is interest in the possibility of standardizing the aboriginal language Guarani. In the standardization process an attempt is made to establish a single norm for pronunciation, grammar, and vocabulary. Interestingly enough, it is in this area that Paraguayan bilingualism approximates diglossia. In Paraguay the language of prestige, Spanish, has already been subject to considerable standardization; it has a well-defined orthography and an established norm for pronunciation, grammar, and vocabulary.

[4] Weinreich, 1953, objected to the use of the term "prestige" for the following attitudes toward a language: (1) The usefulness of a language as a means of communication, (2) The literary-cultural worth of a language, (3) The emotional significance of a language, and (4) The total dominance configuration.

[5] Barker, 1948, suggested that a second potential function of a language in a bilingual situation was its symbolization of an individual's status in a new society.

[6] Gardner and Lambert, 1959, also isolated these two functions and designated them as "instrumental" and "integrative".

[7] This term was suggested by Garvin and Mathiot, 1960. Ferguson, 1959a, called this attitude "standardization".

In contrast, the other language in Paraguay, Guarani, operates much like the other or "lower" variety of diglossia in that there has been little agreement with respect to these linguistic features.

In the literature a number of social variables operating to determine usage have been isolated. For diglossia situations, Ferguson, 1959a, suggested that the opposition "formality-informality" determines which variety should be used. In a more general sense, Haugen, 1956, mentions family, neighborhood, church, occupation, age, race, and political affiliation as possible social variables determining choice of usage. However, social variables determining usage change with each bilingual community and with different social situations. Two other sources provide a broad review of the range of domains which might determine usage: Fishman, 1964, and Ervin-Tripp, 1964.

I feel my analysis of usage makes an important contribution to understanding the nature of social variables in socio-linguistic studies. I have not only isolated the variables determining language usage but I have also specified the hierarchical order in which these variables are to be considered. In addition, the analysis not only spells out the ideal patterns of usage but also describes the patterns of individual variation.

The area of acquisition and proficiency has not been discussed in too great detail in the literature. However, most current scholars would agree that a bilingual need not have perfect command of both languages but rather a bilingual can be defined as an individual who has learned some of the elements of the second language or dialect (Weinreich, 1951 and 1953; Haugen, 1956; Diebold, 1961b). This is an extremely useful definition because it allows us to understand the process of becoming a bilingual and focuses on the ability to communicate instead of on the perfection of the linguistic skill. While agreement on the concept of a bilingual is available, satisfactory methods for measuring relative proficiency have not yet been established. Such methods should allow for a description of all degrees of bilingual skill.[8]

Writers have suggested that in any analysis of the acquisition and proficiency of second languages, two important social variables are age and sex. In my analysis of Paraguayan language competence I have not only used these two but have added an examination of the importance of other social factors in the acquisition of, and proficiency in, both languages of Paraguay. In the literature emphasis has been placed not only on the age of learning but also on the manner in which each language is acquired because "the aptitudes, opportunities and motivations for learning at various ages are so different" (Haugen, 1956). Diebold, 1962, found that bilingualism was correlated with age and sex among the Huave. Bilingualism was found to be

---

[8] Diebold, 1961b, suggested a tripartite scale to indicate the approximate relative bilingual ability of a speaker by comparing the proficiency of speakers in each language. He used the following terms: incipient bilingual, subordinate bilingual, and coordinate bilingual. Although this scale is unique in its kind and while it is extremely useful to think of the process of becoming a bilingual in these terms, the actual techniques used for gathering the data were based on the ability to translate a vocabulary list. The ability to translate, Diebold recognizes, is not coterminous with other linguistic skills; the need for measurement techniques is still very pronounced.

predominantly a male adult or male adolescent skill. He found that these skills "taken together indicate that the majority of bilinguals will not pass on this linguistic heritage to their children" (p. 29).

Finally, my fourth factor, stability, is an area which requires a great deal of research. Several suggestions have been made in the literature concerning both the reasons for the maintenance or disturbance of the bilingual equilibrium and the means to measure whether the situation is indeed stable.

When the speakers of two or more languages come into contact some adjustment in communication must occur. As indicated above, one of the languages may continue and the others die out, or some or all of the languages may persist. If two or more persist, then some equilibrium will be established for a period of time. The term equilibrium may refer to the ratio of bilingual to monolingual speakers or to the distributional patterns of usage. Changes in the ability ratio may affect the degree of interference. Changes in usage may enhance a language or cause it to die out. Once an equilibrium is established, the dying out of one of the languages must reflect a profound cultural change. As Swadesh, 1948, indicated: "Of all the cultural facts that identify and characterize a community, language is one of the more deep-seated and persistent" (p. 234).

In order to ascertain those factors affecting the bilingual equilibrium, it is necessary first to examine the socio-economic factors responsible for its establishment. Changes in this equilibrium will result from changes in the relation of socio-economic variables. Ferguson, 1959a, suggested several factors fostering change in the diglossia equilibrium: more widespread literacy, greater contact with outside communities using the same language, greater geographic and social mobility, and a desire for a national language. Diebold, 1962, listed three factors maintaining the bilingual equilibrium in his Huave community and preventing its change: endogamy, a dependent nuclear family, and religious and political duties. These suggestions were of help in understanding the long period of Paraguayan bilingual equilibrium.

The phenomenon of code-switching[9] may offer a measure of shift. Code-switching often occurs between individuals who are: (1) completely bilingual and (2) social equals. It is not clear, however, whether code-switching is a temporary phenomenon, indicating a transition in use from one language to another, or whether it is a permanent part of bilingual communities.

This book presents an analysis of Paraguayan bilingualism as revealed principally through discussions of the interrelationships between these four extra-linguistic factors — stability, usage, attitudes, and acquisition and proficiency. In the chapters which follow I will discuss the four factors as they relate to the Paraguayan situation

---

[9] Diebold, 1963, defines code-switching as "successive alternate use of two different languages within the same discourse". A problem arises in observing code-switching in Paraguay because of its use in extremely casual circumstances. It is difficult to make tape recordings of this type of speech because the presence of the recorder cuts down on the possibility of producing such circumstances. Because of the fact that I dealt with a rather large number of people and because of the problems of tape recording, I was only able to observe code-switching in an informal way on rare occasions.

in order to understand more fully the relationship between language behavior and other socio-cultural behavior in a bilingual community . In addition, I will analyze the relationship between these four factors and the history of contact between the languages, the acculturation process occurring within the bilingual community, and the socio-economic structure of the community.

II. HISTORICAL BACKGROUND AND EXPLANATION

Paraguayans are unique in Latin America in the importance they give their aboriginal language, Guarani. In all of the other Latin American countries the Indian language is relegated to a secondary position—it is the language of the lower class or of the still extant aboriginal groups (Cf. Peru, Schaedel, 1959; Mexico, Rowe, 1947). City people either do not know of the existence of many of these languages or, if they admit awareness, they usually deny the importance of the language or its speakers in the main stream of their national culture.

This is not the case in Paraguay. A large segment of the population has a high degree of "language loyalty" (cf. Chapter IV) and discussions about the importance and value of Guarani are easily provoked. The literature is full of references to the importance of Guarani as a symbol of Paraguayan nationalism.

The Guarani language is the national language *par excellence*. It is the one that one speaks by the mere fact of having been born within the bounds of Paraguay. It is the instrument of communication of cultured or uneducated people, of literate or illiterate people (Translated from: Valdovinos, 1945, p. 8).[1]

Even U.S. officials have come to recognize the importance of Guarani. President John F. Kennedy's Inaugural Address of January 20, 1961, reproduced in Guarani by the weekly bilingual tabloid *ACA'Ẽ*, was redistributed in pamphlet form by the U.S. Information Service. The Embassy also sponsors a ten-minute daily news-broadcast in Guarani.

Every president of Paraguay has been able to speak Guarani and many have been known to use the language to gain political favor while campaigning. In the rest of Latin America, presidential knowledge of the aboriginal language is rare. In Mexico, Juarez was famous as *the* president of Indian origin; until he was twelve years old he spoke only Zapotec. In Peru, the dictator Sanchez Cerro was known to have spoken Quechua. Other Latin American examples of this sort of executive bilingual ability have not been encountered.

One Latin American country has a linguistic situation similar to Paraguay. In

---

[1] "La lengua guaraní es la lengua nacional por excelencia. Es la que se habla por el solo hecho de haber nacido dentro de la geografía paraguaya. Es el instrumento de comunicación de la gente culta o inculta, alfabeta o analfabeta." (Valdovinos, 1945, p. 8).

Haiti, the linguistic coexistence of Créole and French seems to produce similar usage (cf. Chapter VII). Here, as in Paraguay, every president has been able to speak both national languages (Cf. Leyburn, 1941, p. 297). Discussions in Haitian literature indicate that at least some authors feel that an identity between Haitian nationalism and the Créole language exists:

... the Haitian nation could not have been born were it not for the Créole language (Translated from: Hyppolite, 1952, p. 5).[2]

However, while the percentages of the total population in Paraguay capable of speaking Guarani (92%) and in Haiti capable of speaking Créole (almost 100%) are both very high, the number of persons capable of speaking Spanish in Paraguay (52%) is much higher than the number capable of speaking French in Haiti (under 15%). Therefore, we may conclude that bilingualism is, in fact, much higher in Paraguay with 52% bilingualism than in Haiti with under 15% bilingualism.[3]

Paraguay is unique in the relationship of the aboriginal language to Spanish, the language of the conquerors. Only in Paraguay has the aboriginal language achieved some national importance. This unique position raises several questions. Why hasn't Spanish assumed the prestige position and become the dominant language in Paraguay? Why do some Paraguayans identify their national spirit with Guarani? What historical, geographical, or social factors have contributed to this uniqueness? A comparison of Paraguay's history and geography with that of the rest of Latin America will help to answer these questions.

In order to limit our discussion, we will start with three assumed preconditions:

(1) A relatively large area.
(2) A relatively homogeneous aboriginal population speaking one language before contact.
(3) The assignment of this area to one country at the time of independence.

As a result of this initial limitation, only five countries in Latin America are found to fulfill all the conditions: Peru, Ecuador, Bolivia, Chile, and Paraguay. All other countries in Latin America either had many different tribes of aboriginals speaking different languages, as in Brazil, Mexico or Guatemala; or the aboriginal group was so small that it died out or disappeared early in the history of the territory, as in Cuba, Costa Rica, Argentina, and Uruguay.

Given these three preconditions, we shall consider the historical process establishing

---

[2] "... le Nation Haitienne n'a pu naître que grace au créole." (Hyppolite, 1952, p. 5).
[3] See *Anuario Estadístico*, 1955, for Paraguayan figures. No census figures on language proficiency are available for Haiti. However, an estimate may be made by using the literacy figures for those ten years and above. These figures constitute an approximation and indicate only some formal exposure to French. According to *Análfabetismo y Nivel de Educación*, Vol. IV (1960), p. 18, of those ten years and above, approximately 10% were literate.

Guarani as the important second language of Paraguay and limiting the importance of the aboriginal languages in the other four countries.

The historical process began with the introduction of a group speaking a language, other than the aboriginal one. In the case of all five countries this language was Spanish. However, from the point of contact on, the histories of these countries began to diverge.

In Paraguay, the initial period of contact was one of constant interaction between the aboriginals and the Spanish. This was largely due to two circumstances: (1) The willingness of the Guarani Indians to collaborate with the Spanish for mutual protection (Service, 1945a, pp. 1-2, 19, 31-32; Gandía, 1939, pp. 33-34) and (2) The high percentage of Spanish-Guarani households established (Washburn, 1871, vol. 1, pp. 57-58; Rubio, 1942, p. 181; Salas, 1958, p. 529). Collaboration between Indians and Spanish in Paraguay dated from the very beginning of Spanish colonization and continued through the initial years of Spanish occupation (Service, 1954a, pp. 271-273).

This mutual cooperation was unique. In Chile, although the small group of Picunche who lived in the North were rapidly subjugated by the Spaniards, the Mapuche, living in the area south of the Bío-Bío River, were not brought under control until sometime in the 1880's (Steward, 1959, pp. 271-273). In Peru, Ecuador, and Bolivia, the general pattern was one of conquest and subjugation with little evidence of collaboration (Steward and Faron, 1959, pp. 155-156).

Paraguay was also noted for the high incidence of marital or concubinal unions which occurred on contact between the Spaniards and the aboriginals. This was due in part to the desire of the Indians to ally with the Spaniards by offering their female offspring and in part to the continued lack of white women willing to leave Spain for this "uncivilized" territory (Salas, 1958, p. 529; Service, 1954a, pp. 32-37). In Chile, however, the Spanish met with resistance, and there was little opportunity for mating with aboriginals. In Peru, Bolivia, and Ecuador, the Spanish were able to attract a large number of Spanish women and there was less intermarriage with the aborigines. The initial period provided many opportunities for the few Spanish men in Paraguay to learn Guarani from their Indian wives.

In addition to the greater initial interaction in Paraguay, the period following contact saw the establishment there of a different kind of social hierarchy and of a different relationship with the Old World. Whereas the western coast was in constant economic and cultural contact with Spain throughout the colonial period, Paraguay was isolated from the mother country. It lacked exploitable natural resources, geographical features made access difficult, and the Spanish imposed artificial restrictions on international trade. There was, however, trade between towns. (Service, 1954a, pp. 26-27). Along with the economic isolation, came the social isolation of the country.

Thus, when a small group of Spanish women arrived at Asunción in 1555, "... a breath of poetry for the romantic conquerors", the frustrated conquistadores discovered that their habitual use of Guarani inhibited their "speaking in Spanish to real ladies dressed in the manner God expected". (Translated from: Gandía, 1932, p. 147).[4]

These "real ladies", however, had little effect on the general character of the town. The mestizo women, whose mothers had been Indians and whose husbands had learned Guarani from their own mothers, continued to teach their children Guarani. As late as 1777, in a report by the Governor of Paraguay, complaints were made to the Spanish crown of the difficulties which the authorities had in communicating with the populace because of its monolingual character (Fernando, 1777, p. 49). Again, in 1791, Peramás noted that even from the pulpit in Asunción, the mysteries of the Catholic religion were explained by popular preference in Guarani, although he reports that the audience was largely bilingual (Peramás, 1946, p. 74).

As a result of the extremely limited immigration and the high percentage of mestizo households, a really insulated upper class, differentiated by language, education, and economic status did not develop in Paraguay. Unknown in Paraguay was the rigid Peruvian association between the élite class and the exclusive use of Spanish.

All agreed to consider themselves equal, without recognizing the status of nobleman or plebian, connections or primogeniture, nor any other distinction than that of being the personnel of a job and that which they carried with them, having more or less a reputation of integrity or talent. It's true that some wanted to distinguish themselves by saying that they descended from the conquerors, from leaders or even from simple Europeans; but no one paid attention to them, nor did they feel prevented from marrying others, or take into consideration the prior position of the mate to be (Felix de Azara, 1847. Translated from: Azara, 1943, p. 195).[5]

Many Indians in Paraguay who did not come into contact with the Spanish settlers did come under the influence of the Jesuit missions, particularly in the isolated area of the Alto Paraná. From 1604 until their expulsion in 1767 the *Compañía de Jesús* worked extensively with the aboriginal population. (Service, 1954a, p. 10). Although on several occasions the Crown requested that the mission schools teach the Indians Spanish, the Jesuits reportedly used only Guarani with the aboriginals and often

---

[4] "Fueron un soplo de poesía para los románticos conquistadores, que a fuerza de chapurrear en guaraní habían perdido la costumbre de tratar con mujeres vestidas como Díos manda y referir a damas auténticas, en sonoro castellano. ..." (Gandía, 1932, p. 147).

[5] "Todos convienen en considerarse iguales, sin conocer aquello de nobles y plebeyos, vínicelos y mayorazgos, ni otra distinción que la personal de los empleos y la que lleva consigo el tener más ó menos caudales ó reputación de probidad ó talento. Verdad es que algunos quieren distinguirse diciendo que descienden de conquistadores, de gefes y aún de simples europeos; pero nadie les hace más caso por eso, ni ellos dejan de casarse, reparando poco en lo que pueda haber sido antes al contrayente." (Azara, 1943, p. 195).

In another document from this period (1797), Governor Lázaro de Riberas reported to the king the strange fact that the conquerors were the ones that adopted the native language rather the reverse:

"Por un fatal desgracia y por varias causas que no se precisa referir aquí, hemos llegado al extremo de que la lengua del pueblo conquistado sea la que domine y dé la ley al conquistador."

even in their own official communications with the authorities (Morínigo, 1959, pp. 237-38; Dominguez, 1918, p. 141). One modern-day historian (Chapman, 1933, p. 115) reported that "At the time of the expulsion of the Jesuits in the eighteenth century, nine thousand volumes were found in nineteen of the missions, of which more than a thousand were in Guarani, ..." In addition to providing education in Guarani for the Indians, the Jesuits took a scholarly interest in the language. In 1624 the Jesuit Antonio Ruiz de Montoya produced an excellent Guarani grammar and dictionary. The Jesuit Pablo Restivo who went to Paraguay in 1691, wrote a Guarani dictionary and later edited Montoya's grammar (see: Restivo, 1722, 1892; Ruiz de Montoya, 1876).

Although a Spanish school system would have made the mestizos more familiar with Spanish, none appears to have been available, with the exception of rudimentary Jesuit mission schools and a few private schools in Asunción. In even these, it was reported in 1743, the students preferred punishment due to continued use of Guarani to following the requirement of the teacher to speak Spanish (Cardozo, 1963, p. 145). According to Dominguez, 1897, until the reign of Charles III (1759-1788) there were, to all intents and purposes, no schools. Only during the least quarter of the 18th century did schools begin to appear and by the end of the century, most of the towns are supposed to have had at least one school. But during the rule of Dr. Francia once again the number of schools was greatly reduced (Dominguez, 1946, pp. 127-132; Warren, 1949, pp. 175-176).

In contrast to Paraguayan isolation, Peru, Ecuador, and Bolivia, maintained extensive contact with Spain. The Viceroyalty, one of the two major administrative centers of the Crown in the New World, was located in Peru. There was constant traffic between the mines of Potosí in Bolivia and Spain. An élite developed in these countries, and Spanish was an important distinguishing feature of upper class status. Few of the conquerors bothered to learn the Indian language. In Chile, Spanish continued as the settlers' only language while the isolated bellicose aboriginals retained their own language.

There is an additional historical question to be considered: What are the reasons for the persistent importance of Guarani, from the time of independence on into the twentieth century?

In 1809, Azara noted the continued use of Guarani in Paraguay, even in government and contrasted this usage with the importance of Spanish in Argentina (Azara, 1943, p. 195). If the report of Carlos R. Centurión is accurate, at the moment of independence in 1811, the founders of the Republic of Paraguay recognized the emotional value of Guarani.

In 1811, it served the Patrician in the weaving of the plot that produced the independence. In this eternal language, in low voices, spoke Fulgencio Yegros and Pedro Juan Caballero. It served to express the sacred ire of Vicente Ignacio Iturbe in the Governor's mansion. In Guarani the password was uttered which opened the doors of the barracks of the Rivera to our liberators. And it was in the vernacular language that the people of May first sang their feeling for country and their faith in the eternal destiny of the new nation (Translated from: C. R. Centurión, 1957, vol. 1, p. 77).[6]

This extended use of Guarani by the founders of the Paraguayan nation is not well documented by Centurión. However, it does seem likely that Guarani was used by educated men to (1) discuss very private matters (2) express extreme anger and (3) express great emotions. There are many influential men in Asunción today who might use the aboriginal language in just these situations.

Although the founders probably used Guarani in the abovementioned situations some appear to have recognized the importance of Spanish. In instructions to schoolteachers by the governmental junta of 1812, they advised the teachers to make sure Spanish was the classroom language and that Guarani be banished from school usage (*Instrucciones para los maestros* ..., 1812).

The British traveler Robertson also indicated that in 1815 distinguished Paraguayans visiting him in Corrientes spoke first in Spanish but soon set it aside to relax in Guarani (Robertson, 1920, p. 104). Thus, it appears that from the beginnings of Paraguay as a nation, Guarani has had a place in the speech of influential Paraguayans. The resulting division in usage between Spanish and Guarani was perpetuated by the relative isolation which marked Paraguayan history into the twentieth century.

Following Independence in 1811, Paraguayan leaders tried to establish relations, both economic and political, with their neighbors and some European countries. But the difficulties encountered led Dr. Francia, then dictator of the country, to close the country to all outside contact, thus preventing the economic and social development which might have come with the release from Spanish dominion.

The isolation of Paraguay in 1823 was almost complete. No commercial relations were maintained with the outside; commerce was reduced to the exchange of a few products in the port of Pilar, and navigation was reduced to the occasional arrival of a boat which had obtained special permission from the "Supreme". There were no political relations with the outside, the government of Paraguay neither sent nor received representatives (Translated from: Chaves, 1942, p. 279).[7]

Cultural contact with the outside appears to have declined or stopped during Francia's era. The school system functioned on a limited scale or not at all. No newspapers

---

[6] "En 1811, sirvió al patricio para urdir la trauma que nos dio la independencia. En esa lengua eterna, en voz baja, hablaron Fulgencio Yegros y Pedro Juan Caballero. Sus giros sirvieron para expresar la ira sagrada de Vicente Ignacio Iturbe en la casa del Gobernador, y en guaraní se dijo el 'santo y sena' que abrió las puertas del Cuartel de la Rivera a las hacedores de nuestra libertad. Y fué en la lengua vernácula que el pueblo de mayo cantó, por la primera vez, su emoción de patria y su fé en el destino perenne de la nueva nación." (C. R. Centurión. 1957, 1, p. 77).

[7] "El aislamiento del Paraguay en 1823 era casi total. No se mantenía vinculación comercial alguna con el exterior, reduciéndose el comercio al trueque de unos pocos productos en Pilar, y la navegación, a la llegada a dicho puerto de un barco por rara excepción política con el exterior, el gobierno paraguayo no enviaba representantes ni los recibía. Desde Nicolás de Herrera, en 1813, ningún plenipotenciario llegó a Asunción; los enviados de Artigas y del Congreso de Tucumán ni siquiera pisaron el suelo guaraní." (Chaves, 1942, p. 279).

or books were published in Paraguay nor could any be imported (Dominguez, 1918, pp. 145-146).

The death of Francia in 1840 marked the beginning of a new era. The succeeding dictator, Carlos Antonio López, tried to encourage commerce, to establish diplomatic relations, to encourage immigration and to reestablish the school system. His efforts at reestablishing the schools were successful even though the level of instruction was not very high. There is no data from official records indicating the prescribed language of instruction or whether the teachers were to try to inculcate any dislike of Guarani. However, in the memoirs of the writer, Juan Crisóstomo Centurión, born in 1840, there is an indication that at least in some schools, the use of Guarani was severely punished.

In school the use of Guarani in class hours was prohibited. To enforce this rule, teachers had distributed to monitors bronze rings which were given to anyone found conversing in Guarani ... on Saturday, the return of the rings was requested, and each one caught with a ring was punished with four or five lashes (Translated from: J. C. Centurión, 1894, p. 62).[8]

However, sanctions such as these were probably only effective in the better schools of Asunción, while in most rural schools Guarani probably remained the main language.

López was followed in 1862 by his military-minded son, Mariscal López, who in 1864, plunged Paraguay into one of the most astonishing wars Latin America has ever seen — Paraguay against the Triple Alliance of Brazil, Uruguay and Argentina. One of the rallying forces of this war is said to have been the use of Guarani as a symbol of Paraguayan unity in the face of the enemy.[9]

At the close of the war, Argentina and Brazil controlled Paraguay. Many Paraguayans who had been in exile during the regime of the Lópezes or who had gone to Argentina for an education returned. They brought with them a more worldly point of view and many acquired the Argentinian disdain toward the aboriginal language. These men were active in the new provisional government and their disdain of Guarani shows up in the description of the proceedings of the 1870 Constitutional Congress. When the representative from Paraguari, a small town in the interior, moved that Congress members be permitted to use Guarani if they so desired, the response was "a general hilarity" and the motion

... was fought energetically by the deputies ... who requested not only that it be rejected, but also that in the future the suggesting of such a motion be forbidden. The Assembly

[8] "Se prohibía hablar en ella, en las horas de clase, el *guaraní*, y a fin de hacer efectiva dicha prohibición, se habían distribuido a los *cuidadores* o fiscales unos cuantos anillos de bronce que entregaba el primero que pillaba conversando en *guaraní*. Este lo traspasaba a otro que hubiera incurrido en la misma falta y así sucesivamente, durante toda la semana hasta el sábado en que se pedía la presentación de dichos anillos, y cada uno de sus poseedores como incurso en el delito, llevaba el castigo de cuatro o cinco azotes. ..." (Centurión, 1894, p. 62).

[9] Cf. C. F. Centurión, 1947, vol. 1, p. 75: "The War of 1864 to 1870 was nourished by the sonorous harmony of the autochthonous language. It was the language in which the women of the 'residenta' cried and in which the men of our land hated and fought." (La guerra de 1864 a 1870 se nutrió con la sonora armonía del idioma autóctonono. Era la lengua en que lloraban las mujeres de la 'residenta' y en la que odiaban y peleaban los varones de nuestra tierra).

by a vote of two -thirds of its members, voted its rejection in the terms suggested (Translated from: Decoud, 1934, p. 179).[10]

This infiltration of Argentinian-educated leaders and the influence of many new teachers from Argentina created a self-consciousness in the Paraguayans of Asunción. For many years, everything Argentinian was emulated — the school system, the civil code, the judicial system. For many years all of the schoolbooks were shipped directly from Buenos Aires without adaptation to Paraguayan history or culture. (Many Latin Americans are surprised to learn that Paraguay still has exactly the same civil code as Argentina). Rejection of Guarani was probably continued until at least the beginning of the 1932 Chaco War.

During the sixty-two years between the War of the Triple Alliance and the Chaco War, 1870-1932, there was an increase in the number of schools and the Spanish language was emphasized (Cardozo, 1965, p. 132). In many Asunción homes, children were forbidden to learn Guarani. It appears that this disdain was an upper class attitude, imposed on the school system (*Revista de Turismo*, 1942, p. 8).

In 1894, Manuel Dominguez, head of the Ministry of Education, and a man who was very interested in the development of Paraguayan schools, referred to Guarani "as a great enemy of the cultural progress of Paraguay".[11] Nonetheless, the majority of the rural or interior inhabitants who had little contact with Asunción or with the few available schools, continued to speak Guarani most of the time. At this time a general association of Guarani with rural or uneducated persons was commonplace. At the same time that these attitudes were prevalent, considerable literature in Guarani, especially poetry, began to appear. Some of the authors were prominent Paraguayans. Among the most outstanding works were two by Narciso Colman: a book of verse, *Ocara Poty*, and an epic poem *Ñande Ypycuera* (Our Ancestors). As early as 1899, Silvano Mosqueira translated some of Becquer's poems into Guarani and in 1927, Leopoldo A. Benitez translated the national anthem into Guarani.

Up to the Chaco War of 1932-35, an ambivalent attitude toward Guarani appears to have prevailed. The upper classes, trying to emulate the cosmopolitan values instilled in them by their Argentinian contacts, looked down upon those who spoke only Guarani. In spite of the strong association between good breeding and the use of Spanish which was formed in the period before the War, most upper class members had, however, known Guarani from childhood. But during this War the government (for security reasons) prohibited the use of Spanish on the battlefield and an association between Paraguayan nationalism and the Indian language is said to have been

---

[10] "... fué combatida enérgicamente por los diputados ... que pidieron no tan sólo su rechazo, sino que se prohibiera terminantemente a que en lo sucesivo fuese promovido el asunto. La Asamblea, por mayoría de los dos terceras partes de sus miembros votó el rechazo, en los terminos propuestos." (Decoud, 1934, p. 179).
[11] "... en 1894 denunció al guaraní como a gran enemigo del progreso cultural del Paraguay." (Cardozo, 1959, p. 82).

reinforced. It is claimed that use of Guarani made the troops feel that they were defending the essence of what was uniquely Paraguayan and it helped mold them together against all opposition (*Revista de Turismo*, 1942, p. 9, and private conversations).

It is significant that in this period, the Guarani theater gained immediate popularity. At a 1933 performance of "Guerra Ayaa" by the leading Guarani dramatist Julio Correa, the theater was so crowded that the police had to be called to help close the doors. Indicative of upper class appreciation of the work of Correa is a letter written to him by the Mayor of Asunción, Bruno Guggiari, in 1933.

Your new dramatic play is a valuable and laudable work of the theater, genuinely national, which makes you worthy of the most heartfelt congratulations and worthy of the great triumph which you achieved last night at your opening. (Translated from: Guggiari, 1933.)[12]

Correa continued his playwriting through the 40's. He died in 1953 and since then the Guarani theater has been relatively inactive.

After the Chaco War, Paraguayan contact with other nations seems to have increased considerably with a resultant emphasis on Spanish. According to Professor Decoud Larrosa, occupant of the Chair of Guarani at the University of Asunción in 1960, feelings toward Guarani in Asunción in the 40's continued to be very negative, even though there still was a very high incidence of monolingual Guarani speakers in the country and a high percentage of bilinguals in Asunción itself.

In the past ten years, there has been an increased interest in Guarani. This "renaissance" has in large part been sponsored by the government. In 1950, the Association of Guarani Writers was formed to encourage writers to use the indigenous language. In 1960, a research group studied the problems of teaching in Spanish to monolingual Guarani children. Although this report was not published and is little known, the Ministry of Education no longer advises teachers to exercise sanctions against the use of Guarani, but rather suggests a gradual transition from Guarani to Spanish. (This does not mean that the exercises are in Guarani but that Guarani is used to explain the Spanish exercise).

In summary, it appears from the available historical data that Guarani has continued to play an important role in Paraguay since Independence and on into the twentieth century for three main reasons:

(1) a negative one — the continued isolation during the 19th century and the failure to develop into an industrial society involved in world trade.

(2) a positive association between Guarani and Paraguayan nationalism demonstrated during two major crisis situations — the War of 1865 and the Chaco War.

[12] "Su nueva comedia dramática, es una valiosa y loable obra de teatro genuinamente nacional, que le hace a Usted digno de las más efusivas felicitaciones y del gran triunfo que obtuvo anoche en su estreno." (Guggiari, 1933).

(3) a division of functions between the two languages which was maintained by the isolation.

The analysis of these functions and the attitudes toward the two languages extant today will be discussed in Chapter IV on Attitudes and Chapter VII on Usage.

III. SOCIO-CULTURAL SETTING

The site of the major portion of the fieldwork was in the district of Luque in the *Departamento Central* (A departamento is the approximate equivalent of an American state). The Luque district consists of the municipality, also called Luque, and the rural area surrounding Luque which is divided into twelve *compañías*. The specific sites of study were the municipality of Luque and one *companía*, Itapuami.[1]

The area has a humid subtropical climate with no dry season. It is situated in a plains zone at an altitude of approximately 150 meters. The rural area of Luque is covered by palm trees, low lying shrubs, tall grasses, and rushes. A marshland borders nearby Lake Ypacarai. (See: Map 1, Luque District). The climate in the winter is usually mild, except for short periods (3 days to a week) of freezing weather. The summers tend to be very hot (ranging from 85°F to around 105°F).

This area was selected for the present study for several reasons:

(1) Because of its proximity to Asunción, (Luque is approximately sixteen kilometers northeast of the capital), the town offered an opportunity for the study of cultural patterns which would reflect those of the big city. Almost twenty-five percent of the town population travel daily to Asunción. Among these are government workers, factory workers, servants, *revendedores* (resellers), and students. Many Luqueños also visit frequently with relatives or friends who live in Asunción. People from the rural area of Luque often send their children to Asunción to obtain a better education.

(2) Because of its location between the rural area and Asunción, the town of Luque offered an opportunity for the study of transitional patterns. In addition to the transitional or intermediate position of the town with regard to cultural patterns, the area of Luque provides the intermediate case in linguistic skills. According to the 1951 census, the frequencies of bilinguality in Paraguay were as follows:

Asunción	76% bilingual
Luque	60% bilingual
All interior (including Luque)	49% bilingual

---

[1] In collecting census data for these areas, two different procedures were used. In Itapuami, the entire population was sampled; it consisted of 1349 persons living in 257 houses. In the town of Luque, a random sample served as the basis for the census; it consisted of 429 inhabitants living in

(3) The size of the town, approximately 11,000, permitted the examination of a variety of linguistic patterns and consideration of relevant economic, social, educational, and other variables.

(4) The rural area of Luque is typical of most of the densely populated area surrounding Asunción. The *compañía* selected as representative, Itapuami, was the one farthest from the town of Luque. This *compañía* seemed to reflect the standard rural patterns of the central area. As Service, 1954b, points out, the homogeneity of rural Paraguay is striking; therefore, in the choice of site, the usual question of sectional differences does not arise.

According to the official census taken in 1950, the district of Luque had 20,196 inhabitants. In 1957, the Malaria Eradication Commission reported that the district had 26,668 inhabitants. For the town itself, in 1957, the Commission reported a population of 8,246 persons. As a result of updating these figures, the population of the town of Luque was estimated at approximately 11,069 inhabitants in 1960.[2] The population of Compañía 9, Itapuami, in 1960 was 1,349 inhabitants living in 257 houses. This figure was the result of the house to house census I made.

The town of Luque, situated in the most heavily populated area of Paraguay, is the fifth largest city in the country (See: Map 2, Population Density). It is built on the central plaza plan with the streets laid out orthogonally. In the middle of the central plaza is the district Catholic church. The buildings around the plaza include the municipal building (which serves as the administrative center during the day, the site of one of the secondary schools during the evening, and the site of many local cultural events), the parish house, the mother house of the only Paraguayan order of nuns, (the nuns run a religious school here, too), Luque's only hotel (The Hotel Iris), a branch of the National Bank and several stores and private residences. A second plaza is located one block away. Facing on it are the police station and police quarters, and many stores and residences. There is also a town well in this

---

72 houses. In addition, the Luque data picture was filled in through informal observations and a study of the town as a unit. These observations did not however enter in the figures when given in the text for the random sample.

[2] In order to update the 1957 figure to the period of investigation, 1960-61, the following procedure was used: (1) Population was calculated on the basis of the number of houses in the town. Most of the numbering of the houses was carried out by the Commission. The central area of the town, which had not been numbered by the Commission, had been numbered by the Municipality. I then added another 300 houses as an estimate of the number of unnumbered new houses built since 1957. The number of houses in the town was then estimated at 2073. (2) The number of inhabitants per house was fixed at 5.34. This figure was based upon two sources — the Malaria Commission inhabitant/house ratio for the town in 1957, and my 1960 inhabitant/house ratio based on a random sample. The Luque figures are based on a sample of 72 houses with 429 inhabitants. (3) The town of Luque was based on the pre-1959 definition of a municipality: that area one kilometer from the church plaza in any direction plus the populated area of the *barrio* of Julio Correa which extends four blocks beyond the one kilometer limit. This was included and used because it is the definition used by the Malaria Commission in numbering the houses.

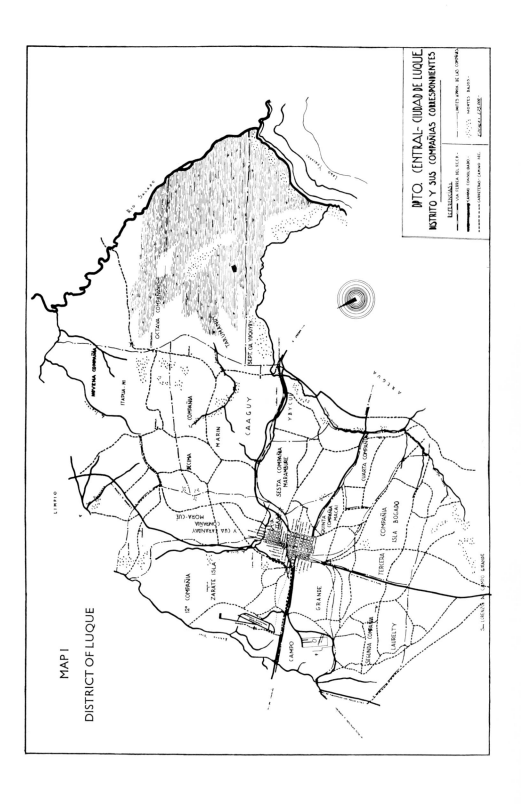

MAP I

DISTRICT OF LUQUE

DTO. CENTRAL- CIUDAD DE LUQUE
DISTRITO Y SUS COMPAÑIAS CORRESPONDIENTES

REFERENCIAS

VIA FERREA DEL RECEP — LIMITES APROX. DE LAS COMPAÑIAS
CAMINO CONSOLIDADO MONTES BAJOS
CARRETERAS: CAMINO SEC. ESCALA 1/25.000

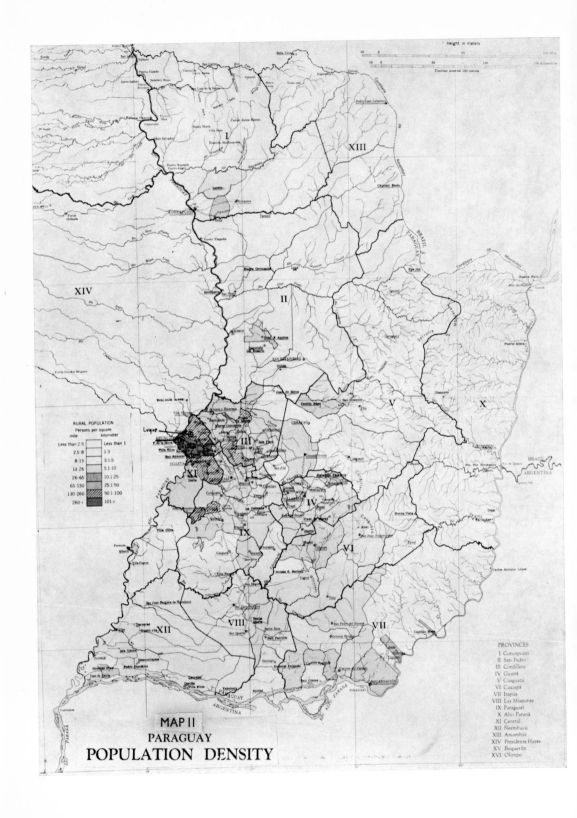

MAP II
PARAGUAY
POPULATION DENSITY

RURAL POPULATION
Persons per square
mile   kilometer

Less than 2.5	Less than 1
2.5-8	1-3
8-13	3.1-5
13-26	5.1-10
26-65	10.1-25
65-130	25.1-50
130-260	50.1-100
260+	101+

Height in meters

Contour interval 100 meters

PROVINCES
I Concepción
II San Pedro
III Cordillera
IV Guairá
V Caaguazú
VI Caazapá
VII Itapúa
VIII Las Misiones
IX Paraguarí
X Alto Paraná
XI Central
XII Ñeembucú
XIII Amambay
XIV Presidente Hayes
XV Boquerón
XVI Olimpo

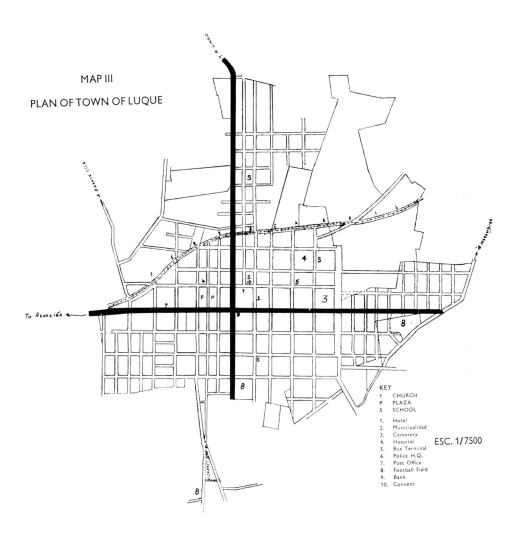

MAP III

PLAN OF TOWN OF LUQUE

To Asunción ←

KEY

† CHURCH
P PLAZA
S SCHOOL

1. Hotel
2. Municipalidad
3. Cemetery
4. Hospital
5. Bus Terminal
6. Police H.Q.
7. Post Office
8. Football Field
9. Bank
10. Convent

ESC. 1/7500

plaza. The town cemetery, the market place, the public hospital, consisting of several one story buildings, and the various public schools are located several blocks from the central plaza (See: Map 3, Town of Luque).

As one moves away from the central plaza, one finds that the streets are less well laid out conforming, in general, to the contour of the land. Most of the streets are not paved. However, the road connecting Luque with Asunción is asphalted and the continuation of this road in Luque (from the point of entry around the central plaza and down to the bus terminal) is cobblestoned. The road to Asunción is paved only because it serves the important function of connecting Asunción with the main national airport and the main military airport. The other roads in Luque are dirt roads, some of which have been leveled; others have deep gullies caused by rain.

Street lights are found on the paved streets in Luque within a two-or three-block radius of the central plaza. Electricity is available for the houses in the older central areas of the town and most people have electricity even though it is very expensive. The areas peripheral to the central plaza and the newer *barrios* (neighborhoods) do not have electricity in the streets or in the houses. Instead, people usually have one or more Coleman lamps; some of the poorer residents have only locally made lamps which yield a very poor light.

Since 1959, the town of Luque has been defined as that area which is three kilometers in any direction from the plaza on which the Catholic church is located. The twelve *compañías* which make up the rest of the district do *not* seem to have extremely well-defined boundaries. Each *compañía* has several different names, depending upon the geographic point used as reference.

Itapuami is situated eight kilometers northeast of the town of Luque. There is a fairly good dirt road leading to the area but the continuation of the road through the *compañía* is so rough that only jeeps can travel it successfully, even in dry periods. The road leads out to bogs and marshes which are the boundaries of the area. In addition to this road, there are also several paths, traversable only on foot or on horseback. The houses are scattered along this road and the paths. The heaviest concentration is along the main road. Ground in this area is fairly wet, and the area is dotted with bogs, marshes, and lagoons. There is a stream which divides the district of Luque from that of Limpio.

Community buildings in Itapuami consist of the three-room school and a small one-room Seventh Day Adventist Church. The school has its own grassy fenced-in yard as well as a separate outhouse. The church was built by the Asunción parish on land given by one of the rural members. There is no market in Itapuami, nor in any of the *compañías*. Meat, slaughtered daily, is sold at several sheds throughout the area. Other goods are available at the very small stores scattered throughout the area. Several of these stores have *caña* (whiskey) for sale and the gentlemen of the area visited there, sitting on benches out of doors, chatting or playing cards.

As we have indicated above, Paraguay presents a very homogeneous cultural picture. Throughout the country male-female roles offer little opportunity for choice;

religion is largely Catholic even though often nominally; there are two major parties in constant dissent and everyone offers similar arguments concerning the advantages and disadvantages of the two. However, in spite of these similarities, many socio-cultural differences may be observed between the central area of the town of Luque and the rural area of Itapuami. In general, the differences between the two areas may be attributed to and measured by the number and kinds of cultural alternatives available to individuals; in the rural areas the variety and number of alternatives is more limited, whereas, this variety increases as one moves toward Luque and expands even more as one moves toward the urban area of Asunción. Probably the biggest differential in number and kind of alternatives is between three or four major cities (Asunción, Concepción, Villarrica, and Encarnación) and the rest of the country. The rest of the country offers alternatives to the individual but the kind and number are quite severely restricted. The differences between the central area of Luque and the rural area of Itapuami are a result of several factors: The amount of contact with urbanites, the availability and quality of education, the amount of access to mass media, and differential wealth and status, due in large part to occupational opportunities.

Communication and transportation facilities permit the town of Luque to maintain easy daily contact with Asunción. Newspapers, published in the capital, are delivered to subscribers and are on sale in the streets every morning. Mail is delivered daily to the local post office station and regular recipients get their mail at home. Magazines local and Argentinian, are on sale at the town variety shops. There is a central telephone office available for calls within the country; in addition, there are seven other instruments, including those in the police station and the Municipal building. There are two movie houses in the town: one, the Marconi, presents films concurrently with the major downtown theaters in Asunción. The other, the Florida, tends to show older movies. A high percentage of the population own their own battery-operated radios.[3] Of the 72 houses included in the random sample, 58 had radios. Almost every bar and shop has a radio; proprietors often play them in order to attract customers. Public announcements are usually made by loud speaker. The Florida theater has a permanent loud speaker over which announcements and advertisements are broadcast every afternoon. Daily news is brought in by the commuters from Asunción.

Access to Asunción is by bus, microbus jitney, auto, truck, and train. The trip by bus usually takes an hour because there are many stops while the trip by jitney and auto takes something under half an hour. On every day except Sunday, there were 34 regular bus trips between Luque and Asunción, with half as many on Sunday.

[3] By 1965, cheap transistor radios were available throughout the country and there was a marked increase in the number of instruments to be found everywhere. This innovation may indeed serve as one of the most important links between the rural area and Asunción. That is for the first time, to a limited extent, the urban area is penetrating the rural area. Living in the country for most urbanites is unthinkable; relatively few rural inhabitants return there after living in the city; thus the effect of the urbanites on rural inhabitants has been quite limited.

In 1961, the jitney regularly made twenty trips a day to the capital. However, the number of trips seemed to be increasing daily as the convenience of the microbus was recognized. The train schedule is much less frequent than it used to be. Formerly it was the major means of transportation; now since the increase of road traffic the number of regular trains passing through Luque on the way to Asunción has been reduced to one or two daily. Although no official figures were available for the traffic between Asunción and Luque, I calculated that approximately 2680 persons travelled daily to Asunción by bus, microbus jitney, train, or private car.

In contrast to Luque's easy and continual access to Asunción, Itapuami's communication with Luque or Asunción is relatively limited. Mail, newspapers, and magazines are not delivered or sold in Itapuami and are available only occasionally when someone brings them from town. There are no movies or telephones and those in Luque are rarely used. The only continuous contact with Asunción is through radio programs. As mentioned above the number of radios is on the increase since the introduction of transistor radios in 1964. In 1961, of 257 households there were only 22 radios and not all of these were operational because the batteries had run down and had not been recharged. In 1965, over 40% of the *compañía* had working radios in their houses.

Although Luque is close to many other towns (San Lorenzo, Trinidad, Aregua, Limpio) most of its business and social contacts are with the capital. This is also true of most other towns in Paraguay. In order to reach other towns by public transportation it is usually necessary to pass through Asunción. However, some people do visit their relatives in these towns and often go on foot or on horseback through the muddy back roads. Regular daily buses between the town of Luque and its *compañías* are available in those areas where a road has been built and is usable. Although Itapuami is only eight kilometers from Luque, the regular bus is often delayed because of the poor conditions of the road. Many passengers often end up making the trip on foot. From Luque it is possible to reach each of the *compañías* on foot in an hour and a half or less. Much of the year the roads are too muddy for motor vehicles. Many of the townspeople have relatives in the rural areas and visit them on weekdays or holidays. On the other hand, since the town tends to have more social activities and religious festivals, the greater tendency is to visit from country to town.

Learning seems to be generally respected in Paraguay. Most people want their children to finish at least three grades of primary school which permits them to be almost functionally literate (read and write some Spanish and do simple arithmetic). For the poorer people, sending children to school constitutes a real sacrifice because of the expense involved. Not only must the parent provide school books and supplies but also a clean white uniform for daily wear in the classroom. From time to time the school requests donations from the parents for supplies (such as chalk) not provided by the Ministry of Education. Most schools have some sort of social event to raise funds for these "necessities". In the country areas the parents are expected to provide labor in order to maintain the school in good repair and to help build benches, chairs, and additional rooms.

The number of people getting an education seems to be increasing. From the censuses of both Luque and Itapuami, it is clear that an increasing proportion of the population does attend school (See: Chapter VI for statistics). Although women have always received some education, it appears that it was always less than that which the men received. This is particularly true in the rural area:

(1) Of the women in the age group 41 and over in Itapuami, 64% had not attended school, whereas, of the men in this age group only 21% had not attended school.

(2) Of the women in the age group 17-40 in Itapuami, 21% had not attended school, whereas, of the men in this age group only 11% had not attended school.

(3) Similar differences between men and women occurred in Luque. However, while women have always received less education, my figures show that their education is rapidly catching up with that of the men.[4]

In Luque, the government maintains three elementary schools (grades 1-6), and two secondary schools (grades 7-12). In addition, the nuns maintain primary, secondary, normal, and "profesorado" schools. Several other private schools exist in the town although on a very small scale. Children of the wealthier families attend school in Asunción. Some of these attend primary schools in Luque but go on to private secondary schools in the capital.

The largest primary school in Luque operates a triple session schedule — morning, afternoon, and evening. Generally the evening session is for poor children who must work during the day and who can only be spared during the evening. As a result of the reduced number of hours, their curriculum is considerably condensed and the students are not expected to maintain the same standard as the day students. One school is known for its attempt to maintain high standards and for its attempts to accept only those students who live in the town. The other primary schools have

---

[4] The figures to support these percentages are as follows:

TABLE 1

Comparison by sex and age of school attendance in Itapuami and Luque in raw scores and percentages (corrected to nearest hundredth).

	Itapuami		Luque (Random Sample)	
	Men (41+) (N=90)	Women (41+) (N=139)	Men (41+) (N=23)	Women (41+) (N=43)
No School	19 (21%)	89 (64%)	1 (4%)	7 (16%)
Some School	71 (79%)	50 (36%)	22 (96%)	36 (84%)

	Itapuami		Luque (Random Sample)	
	Men (17—40) (N=186)	Women (17—40) (N=229)	Men (17—40) (N=57)	Women (17—40) (N=75)
No School	21 (11%)	49 (21%)	0 (0%)	4 (5%)
Some School	165 (89%)	180 (79%)	57 (100%)	71 (95%)

some students who come to town every day to go to school, some because of the inferiority of the country schools and others because many of the rural schools only have classes through the third grade. The nuns' school draws mainly paying students. Its standard is high because the students have more time to give to their studies and because parental interest seems to be greater.

The two universities of Paraguay are located in Asunción and several of the young people of the town commute regularly to attend classes.

The Itapuami school has four teachers who hold two sessions a day. Because the school only offers five grades, those who desire to complete primary school must travel to town to do so. Classes are quite large in the first two grades, but decrease as the grades advance.

The town of Luque is famous for its many products. The importance of particular products has varied from year to year, but the most commonly produced articles are: gold jewelry, ready-made clothing, luggage, straw hats, shoes, tailor-made clothing, bluing, and bricks. Many food products are prepared in Luque for sale in Asunción. These include: candy, delicatessen articles, manioc flour, oil, bread, whiskey, and spaghetti. A large part of the town is engaged in this sort of small scale industry and most products are sold or resold in Asunción rather than in Luque. Luque is also known for its large number of orchestras and musicians.

From my random sample of the town, it would appear that most of its inhabitants were not participating in agriculture. However, a few of the men who lived in some of the more peripheral *barrios* (neighborhoods) of the town engaged in some agricultural activities, at least part-time. Although some of the upper stratum owned land which was worked by tenants, they themselves held other positions which occupied most of their time.

The women who worked were usually dressmakers or makers of ready-to-wear garments.[5] Many lower stratum women resell goods in the market in Asunción or in Luque. Others were laundresses or worked as maids or cooks or nurses. Women also helped in small home factories which made food products. Some worked with their husbands in small retail businesses. Several were engaged as teachers; this occupation seemed to be the only profession to which women could aspire.

The occupations of men in Luque were divided among several non-agricultural pursuits. They participated, with women, in the production of foodstuffs, clothing (tailors), and jewelry. Men, alone, produced metal, wood, and leather objects. They provided a variety of services such as those of barber, electrician, mechanic, truck/bus driver, and musician. Some of the men held government jobs in either civil or military capacities. Several professionals lived in Luque including doctors, teachers, pharmacists, lawyers, draftsmen, and a priest.

In contrast to Luque's diversity of occupations, in Itapuami almost everyone was

[5] This parallels the situation reported by Service, 1954b: "The greatest number of women (one hundred and eleven), both single and married, consider themselves seamstresses or needleworkers" (p. 89).

engaged in farming or in making straw hats. It was usually the males who did the farming, although women helped. Making straw hats was a community-wide occupation; women did it whenever they could, while cooking or talking or nursing their child. Many young people did it too and in this way added to the family cash income. Men also wove straw hats in their spare time. For some it was a full-time occupation. Kept occupied in this way, most of the inhabitants remained in the *compañía* and had little reason to go to town on a regular basis. Agriculture was primarily for subsistence purposes.

There were two or three jobs which required a regular trip out of the area. In 1961, ten of the 1349 inhabitants of Itapuami worked in a near-by meat packing factory and returned home only on weekends. Twelve persons were *revendedores* (resellers) and traveled to Luque or to Asunción to sell fruits, vegetables, or dry goods. A couple of people went to town when they had enough of their product (firewood, meat, or hats) to sell. Hats were usually bought in a semi-finished state by one or two stores in Itapuami, finished by them, and then resold to buyers in Luque. Eleven girls were seamstresses and half of them traveled daily to town to get the dozen items to be completed each day.

There were thirteen stores in the area and each owner made a monthly trip to town to stock his store. A few people engaged in other occupations, most of which did not require them to leave Itapuami. These included the barbers, a bricklayer, butchers, and carpenters. There is one "practical" doctor in the community. One man was an overseer of a large estate, much of which was rented out to tenant farmers. Some of the farmers also engaged in part-time occupations in addition to their farming. A couple of men made rope to sell, three men made fire-crackers during the holiday season, one man made straw baskets, and many helped make hats during their spare time.

Thus, few of the inhabitants need to leave Itapuami for business reasons. With the exception of the local school teachers, none of the community members is engaged in a profession. In Itapuami, opportunities for great differences in wealth are not present. Census figures indicate that the area is overpopulated, the land overworked, and there are indications of a continuing decline in agricultural production.

Social relations within both the rural area and the town tend to result most frequently from informal opportunities to associate with family and friends. These usually take the form of spontaneous activities which are normally not highly formalized. They are often done on the spur of the moment and usually do not require a prior appointment. In fact, as a general rule, most Paraguayans do not have or enjoy formal dinners or parties because it obliges them to do more than they can financially afford. They prefer, instead, informal arrangements for which expectations are not too high. A great deal of social life in both areas consists of visiting friends' homes. Usually a group of men will sit around at a friend's house sipping *yerba mate* tea or drinking *caña* and playing a guitar. Women, too, gather in each other's homes to drink hot yerba mate and to chat. Another frequent pastime of young men is sitting around in a bar, talking and drinking. Of course, women are never part of these groups. A young man will court a young women by visiting her in her home and will honor her on special occasions by a serenade sung at her door after bedtime. While these informal groupings are not usually premeditated, rules as to the proper hour and day for such meetings seem to exist. Boys may visit girls on Tuesdays, Thursdays, Saturdays, and Sundays. Men usually visit with their male friends in the evenings and on Sunday mornings. All day Sunday it is common to go visiting. *Mate* drinking is usually done by women in the afternoons, by men in the afternoons and evenings. (Men may also drink *terere*, cold *mate*, which women do not drink). Somewhat more organized activities occur both in the rural area and the town. On such occasions as Saint's days, birthdays, first communions, weddings, baptisms, and funerals, an informal open house is usually held and friends and relatives are expected to call. However, on all of these occasions the number of guests usually is quite unpredictable and may include a wide range of family and friends. In the rural area, activities surrounding death are quite elaborate and include the wake, the burial, and the nine-day novena; participation of family, friends, and neighbors is expected.

Apart from the above-mentioned groupings which occur as a result of little formal organization, the rural area has few other organized activities. In some *compañías*, private individuals will regularly hold paid dances which offer an opportunity for social gatherings. The main object of a dance is to obtain or to entertain a sweetheart. One other popular form of recreation is football (soccor). Within Itapuami, there are several ball fields, used mainly on weekends. Usually the teams are organized into clubs. Such clubs do not, as in Luque, sponsor social events.[6]

In the town of Luque, there are many more formally organized associations around which public activities are centered, and which offer a wider variety of entertainment. First of all, the Catholic church plays a very important role in town life. Nominally the entire community is Catholic. Some citizens participate frequently and actively in church events. Most of these live in the town of Luque. Others participate only in festivals or call on the church for life crisis rituals. All official funerals, weddings, and baptisms in the entire district take place in the church. Of these three, the

---

[6] The only other sort of community activity in rural areas depends on the particular community and the amount of "community spirit" present. In each *compañía* in which there is a school, it is the responsibility of the *compañía* to maintain it in good physical order. A school committee is usually established to help the teacher do so. In some *compañías* there seems to be relatively greater cohesion and considerable cooperative community activity. In others, it is difficult to get any cooperation. School directors are particularly aware of the degree of cohesion. Some found it is almost impossible to get help, while others were always aided. An outstanding example of cooperation was the *compañía* of Marambure. There, people had worked together to build a dirt road to town, to procure a regular bus trip to their area, to build a community chapel, and to construct a bigger school. This cooperative spirit was not, however, greatly in evidence in the *compañía* of Itapuami. In fact, at the beginning of the school year in 1960, in order to enlist the support of the parents, a local police inspector was invited to the parent-teacher meeting to "encourage" the parents to help with the annual clean-up duties. The directoress of the school agreed to my working in the community. but warned that people in general were uncooperative and *koigua* (timid, backward).

funeral is the only life crisis ritual for which all Paraguayans call upon the church. Many ignore the Catholic requirements for baptism and marriage. The local priest works mainly in the town, visiting each *compañía* only two or three times a year. All of the major religious festivals are usually followed or preceded by a procession in the church plaza.

In addition to the many church activities, there are several other associations. Among the most important is the social club called the Centro Balderrama (named after the founder of the city). It has its own buildings and sponsors several social events for members each year. Membership fees, while not expensive by Asunción standards, do limit the Club to the upper stratum of the community. Membership numbers approximately three hundred. Members are expected to maintain certain standards of comportment and may be expelled from the club if they depart from these standards.[7] The president of the club is usually one of the more influential members of the community.

There is another important social club in Luque but its functions are more related to football than to purely social activities. The club has a large membership and its own clubhouse, grounds, and playing field. It, too, sponsors social events. Its annual dance, however, is not exclusively for members; it is open to the entire community. Most Luqueños are very proud of the club and of the record of its team. Fans often follow the team to Asunción for a game, and Asuncenos may follow their own favorite teams to Luque.

In addition to this club, almost every neighborhood has its own local football club. Usually the club consists of just a playing field without a clubhouse. During the year each club usually sponsors at least one social event which is open to the public.

There are a number of other social clubs or associations. Membership in most of these is based on interest rather than on social status. Such clubs include religious associations (such as the Catholic Action or neighborhood patron saints), civic organizations (such as special committees for specific purposes: the Hospital Committee, the Committee for the Patron Saint's Day, the Police Home Committee), literary groups (such as the Friends of Art and a branch of the Association of Guarani Writers), and political organizations (such as *barrio* divisions of the incumbent party and town-wide associations of the opposition), and a number of veterans' groups associated with the Chaco War. In all of these groups, membership may include people from all areas of town and all social classes. Only one is regularly associated with upper stratum people. The Patron Saint's Day Committee usually consists of those persons who are recognized as social and political leaders.

The problem of social status of individuals living in either area must be considered in connection with a number of cultural attributes but we would agree generally with Service, 1954b, that all other things being equal "Town dwellers are, in general considered to be a step above the country people in status, ..." (p. 141). In general

----

[7]   An example of the type of standards set by the club is the exclusion of the female member of a consensual union from official functions of the Club.

these differences are attributable to such cultural attributes as manners and general modern sophistication. The townsman usually places himself above the rural inhabitant because the people in the country do not get as much education as those in town and because little reading matter finds its way to rural areas, so that whatever skills a rural inhabitant may have learned are never exercised. As Service points out it is usually possible to identify rural inhabitants because "The peasant's speech, dress and manners vary from those of the townsmen" (p. 141). People in the rural areas usually are not as competent bilinguals. This seems to be due to the poorer quality of the rural schools and because of the tradition (read: single cultural alternative) of using only Guarani. In the rural area, again as indicated by Service "Family life and respect etiquette are more intense and courtesy and hospitality are more important" (p. 142). In the rural area, residence in close proximity to consanguineal relatives is much more common than in town. Also, the traditional custom of benediction (*tupanoi*) by close ascending generation consanguineals continues in the rural area whenever someone of the descending generation enters a house. Visitors to a rural home are always treated with great respect, are usually offered a snack, and are almost always invited to join in at mealtimes. This is much less the case in the town. Again, countryfolk were always much more anxious than townfolk to include me in their social activities and went out of their way to see that I would attend. That the differences in speech, dress and manners are important in distinguishing social status is indicated by the lack of social ease which rural people have in the presence of townsmen. Naturally, this uneasiness is modified somewhat by the amount of education and linguistic proficiency which a person has, but country people are generally aware that they are being regarded as a notch lower.[8]

Apart from rural-urban differences in consideration of social status, a number of other cultural attributes are important. We agree with Service that "social ranking involves basically two groups: 'society' (la sociedad) and 'the people' (la gente)".[9] However, the dichotomy, relatively clearly marked in Tobatí, is, in Luque, somewhat complicated by the proximity of Asunción. In general, the society of Asunción,

[8]   An expression of their awareness of this difference was the remark of a peasant who noted that it was advisable to speak Spanish when doing business at the municipal office or else the clerks wouldn't pay attention to you. Another demonstration of this awareness is a peasant's refusal to go with me to the house of a friend who had lived in Itapuami but who had grown up in Luque, because the peasant felt "too timid" and thought my friend too upper class.

[9]   This dichotomy was fairly well substantiated in Luque. At a party at the Sport Club honoring one of its departing team members, "society" was seated and served snacks and drinks while "the people" remained standing and bought their drinks outside. The two dance floors, one indoors and one outdoors, furthered the separation of the two groups, although there was some intermingling because of the occasion. This separation irked several business men who had contributed to the party but who had not been invited to join the "elite" group. By this example we can see that while the dichotomy is clearly made, the allocation of specific persons is not always clear cut. On another occasion, at a supper party which I gave for friends in town, I mistakenly "mixed" groups and those in "la gente" class declined to come or came very late just to pay their respects. One of my "gente" friends explained that he couldn't just come because the "gente fifí" (upper class types) would be there. The one person from "la gente" who did come to dinner, after much persuasion, stood in a corner listening to the radio and looking very uncomfortable.

is one or more notches higher than that of Luque. Thus, the relationship between Asunción and Luque is like that of Luque and Itapuami, in that all other things being equal Asuncenos are a notch above Luqueños. Although one may be at the top of Luque society, somehow living in the "country" (for Asuncenos, anyone living outside the city is in the "country") usually lowers one's status a notch, unless one has been born and raised in Asunción and later moved to Luque.

While the dichotomy between "la gente" and "la sociedad" is clearly made, we found as Service did that "In practice, however, the gradation of *individuals* from top to bottom is continuous — sharp distinctions between the two groups are not made" (p. 133). The process of judging individuals as higher or lower in the social ladder, requires some isolable cultural attributes. These are listed by Service for Tobatí and apply as well to Luque to a large extent.

Wealth — In Tobatí symbols which suggest or prove more permanent familial wealth are more significant and indicative of higher social status than symbols of strength which suggest only temporary advance. My observation has been that Luque has a more mobile social group than Tobatí. People in Luque participate more frequently in Asunceno life and as a result, place less emphasis on permanent familial wealth. One did not often hear about the old "aristocratic" families of Luque. Those who had reason to feel "aristocratic" participated in Asunceno society instead of remaining in a closed group within Luque. This contrasts strongly also with the town of Concepción (one of the four major cities in Paraguay) which is quite far removed from the capital and which maintains a tightly knit upper stratum group. The difference between the two cities is probably attributable to the fact that the people of Luque consider any sign of wealth, even though temporary, a basis for the assignment of a person to "la sociedad". However, wealth is not the only way of determining status. If a person has other attributes and relatively little wealth, he might still be considered a part of the upper stratum. In fact, in a definition of "la sociedad" one informant suggested that the criteria for placement in this category were that the individual be: (1) a distinguished person, (2) one who frequented the social clubs, and (3) one who mixed with aristocratic people. The last item refers presumably to contact with Asunción society.

In addition to wealth, occupation is also used as an attribute of social status without regard to the exact earnings of the individual. A professional (doctor, lawyer, CPA, priest) would automatically be put into the "la sociedad" status whereas a manual laborer would be placed in "la gente". Teachers and white collar workers, either military or civil, would probably be placed more frequently higher up in the scale but would not necessarily be part of "la sociedad".

Education — In Tobatí, "education" is the most typical attribute of "society". "Education" refers not only to formal schooling, but also to good breeding. Since formal education is a relatively expensive process, the amount of education a person has is naturally related to the amount of wealth his family has. As a result, in Luque as elsewhere in Paraguay, the upper stratum tends to have more education than the lower. However, since the current trend is toward more education for everyone, a younger person of lower status may have more education than an older person of upper status. People seem to try to make more of a sacrifice now to educate their children and one of the ways of being "upwardly mobile" is to make this effort to give the children a longer formal education. In the upper stratum, the distinguishing attribute is sending children to Asunción to attend private secondary schools, a fairly costly procedure.

Marriage — In Paraguay, there are several different kinds of unions. The one carrying the most prestige is a church ceremony; the next, a civil ceremony, and the least, a consensual union. Status associated with these different kinds of unions, is from highest to lowest, in the above order. It should be noted that this order is from the most permanent to the least permanent. In Tobatí, marriage in the church is rare outside the "sociedad". Members of "la sociedad" in Luque also always have church marriages, but many people of less social status do too. In general, "la gente" seem to be less able to afford church weddings, but it is nonetheless the most desired form. Consensual unions were among the most frequent in the countryside. When, however, the opportunity to legalize these unions presented itself in the form of a visiting church dignitary who offered to perform the ceremony for nothing, many long-standing consensual unions were made legitimate.[10]

Language — All native born Paraguayans can speak Guarani. Census data from 1951 support this since ninety two percent of the country is reported able to speak this aboriginal language. Ability to speak Spanish is not necessarily correlated with an individual's status; among the "la sociedad" of Asunción however, Spanish is the most frequent language. It is possible to use Spanish in almost all situations in Asunción; certainly one who could not maintain a conversation in Spanish would not qualify for membership in Asunción society. In Luque, ability to speak Spanish is certainly almost always a prerequisite for acceptance into "la sociedad". Individuals however, may vary as to their usage preferences.

Another sort of social classification that influences social relations throughout Paraguay, is a differentiation in roles assigned to women and men. In general the double sex standard so common throughout Latin America applies and men are expected to prove themselves by being "macho". Male-female relationships, not related to the family, are considered to exist for the physical aspect alone. Any social intercourse between non-familial men and women is suspect. One male informant felt that women were actually incapable of discussing topics important to men such as politics and religion. To avoid gossip both husbands and wives guard

---

[10] As Service indicated an illegitimate child who is *"reconocido"* ('recognized,' i.e. bears his father's family name) and whose family forms a stable consensual union does not suffer any social stigma" (p. 144). Very "often a man of good family may have one or more children by a lower-class woman before he is married. If he recognizes the child, financial provision is sometimes made to enable the mother to care for it, or the child may be raised in the household of one of the young man's relatives" (p. 144). In general, illegitimate children do not constitute a source of shame even to "la sociedad" members.

against isolated conversations with the opposite sex, although men are permitted much wider latitude than women in this regard. Since dancing is considered primarily an opportunity to "catch" a girl friend, most married women do not dance after marriage. If they do so, it is only with their husbands.

Women are generally much more tied to the house. A woman rarely leaves her home unless she has to go out to work or to market. Many errands are run by small children, thus reducing the number of times she has to leave home. If a woman does go out alone, it is always during the day. No woman would feel safe outdoors alone at night. In addition to fear of male attackers, many women also fear ghosts. Young girls usually ask a companion to go with them on errands requiring only a two or three block walk.

Within the household, it is the man who receives the greatest respect from both his wife and children. When guests are present, the wife and children will usually eat in the kitchen, particularly those in the lower social stratum. An example of this is an elaborate rural party I attended where the men were fed first at a buffet table. When they had finished, the women were invited to go up to the table to serve themselves. This separation is related in part to sex divisions but also in part to the respect accorded men. At another upper stratum party, the men and two honored female guests were served at the dining room table while the women and children ate in the kitchen.

A behavioral result of some of these social differences — class, sex, location — is that between the various groups one can expect more formal behavior, whereas between members of a group both formal and informal behavior can be expected. Formal behavior is clearly distinguishable from informal behavior. Formal behavior involves a stiffness and a reticence to converse, whereas informal behavior includes animated discussions, manifest curiosity, and often a great deal of joking. Manifestations of this formal behavior in Luque, both in the town and in the rural area are seen in the following patterns:

(1) A stranger never enters the yard of a house without invitation. He indicates his presence by clapping his hands and then waits for an invitation. Friends usually wait for an invitation, but if no one answers, they may enter the yard to locate the owner.

(2) A chair is always offered a guest who is a stranger whereas a friend may come and stand or may be expected to find his own chair.

(3) Serving a meal under formal circumstances requires separation of the guest from the family. As mentioned above, in most homes, the family or at least the females will eat apart from the guests. In lower stratum families a guest will be given separate utensils, plates, glasses, and a napkin, whereas a friend will be invited to share dishes, glasses, utensils, and the table-cloth which serves as a napkin. The degree of formal behavior will depend in general upon the status and familiarity of the individuals. However, the occasion and other participants in the action may also determine the behavior.

This discussion of the social setting of Luque and Itapuami has pointed to some of the important variables which affect behavior. It is our intention to consider in the following chapters how these variables and Paraguayan history affect socio-linguistic behavior by shaping attitudes, usage, acquisition and proficiency, and stability.

IV. ATTITUDES

Paraguayans are notable for their expression of concern and interest in their national languages. The highly bilingual nature of the country probably accounts for this overt expression. People constantly talk about the quality of their usage of each language and often criticize the speech of their fellow countrymen. They are deeply interested in the educational and social problems posed by their linguistic duality.

Most speakers are ambivalent in their feelings about the two languages. The bilingual speaker who prefers to use Spanish usually recognizes the importance of Guarani for most of the country. The bilingual speaker who prefers to use Guarani usually recognizes the international importance of Spanish, economically and culturally. Although there are positive attitudes associated with both languages, Spanish tends to be the language which is revered whereas Guarani is frequently belittled. The speaker who can control Spanish is *culto* (educated, civilized), *inteligente* (intelligent), *distintivo* (distinctive), and *desarrollado* (cultured). The man who controls only Guarani is called a *Guarango* (ill-bred type), *menos inteligente* (less intelligent), *menos desarrollado* (less cultured), and *no tiene principios* (does not have [moral] principles). Negative appraisal of the Guarani monolingual is widespread; positive appraisal is unusual. One sophisticated gentleman expressed surprise when he found that one of the most prolific writers of Guarani poetry was a man who had real principles and a well-defined personality. Paraguayans do not expect to find these characteristics in someone who thinks primarily in Guarani. Another educated speaker found it surprising that this poet's work met all the prescribed criteria for good poetic form *even though* it was expressed in Guarani.

Monolingual speakers of Guarani even refer to themselves as *tavi* (stupid) because they are unable to speak Spanish.[1] They consider those who can speak Spanish *iñarandu* (intelligent).

In spite of these negative attitudes toward Guarani, most Paraguayans feel some pride in their bilingualism. Even the most educated Paraguayan feels the impulse occasionally to express some feeling or thought in Guarani. And, if there is some validity in the last census figures indicating that approximately 90% of the population

---

[1] Probably this estimate of themselves is due, too, to the fact that a country person can only learn to speak Spanish in school and thus degree of education and ability to speak Spanish are closely linked in the minds of most rural people.

know how to speak Guarani, then most Paraguayans still must feel the need to use the language. In contrast to the capital cities of Peru and Mexico where the number of inhabitants speaking both Spanish and an aboriginal language is below 10%,[2] the population of Asunción is reported to be 76% bilingual.

It is this ambivalence toward Guarani which will be examined in this chapter. I shall discuss attitudes toward the language and the origins of these attitudes.[3] A clear picture of this ambivalence is presented by the following comments on the two languages made by the assistant director of a high school in one of the larger cities in Paraguay, Concepción.

Undoubtedly, within our own country, we grant that we can use both languages. Obviously, this would at no time be considered bad breeding. On the contrary, it would indicate that we love our language, a thing which is natural. We have no reason at all to reject it. Of course, as someone said, if we are considering a social function, it would surprise us to hear Guarani. But I would at no time consider this inappropriate, nor could I criticize such usage because it is our language.

A. LANGUAGE LOYALTY

As mentioned above, in Paraguay, attacks on language have all been directed at the negative qualities and inadequacies of Guarani, and never at those of Spanish. I found no evidence that Spanish was ever considered inadequate or was attacked; conversely, I found a limited number of cases where Guarani was felt to have superior qualities (see post: Pride). No one has ever suggested that Spanish be eliminated from usage in Paraguay. Such a proposal would be considered ludicrous by even the most ardent Guarani supporters. Since Spanish is never attacked, I found no demonstration of particular loyalty toward Spanish.

In contrast, I did find evidence of continued attack on and defense of the aboriginal language. There is no doubt that at present Guarani is under less attack than it was twenty years ago. This is partly due to the present government's attempted identification of Guarani with the national interest and national character. It is also attributable to the extensive pro-Guarani campaign conducted by the most renowned

---

[2]   According to the Mexican census of 1950, approximately 2% of the population of Mexico City spoke Spanish and an aboriginal language. According to the Peruvian census of 1940, (none was available for 1950) approximately 10% of the population of Lima spoke Spanish and an aboriginal language.

[3]   Evidence for these attitudes were collected from mass media, from types of institutional support or disfavor, from unsolicited remarks made during numerous formal interviews, and from informal interviews. The latter included discussions with a wide range of Paraguayans from intellectual élite in Asunción, to rural schoolteachers, to the man on the street in small towns or the man on the road in the countryside. None of the material on attitudes was collected through systematic interviewing so that no real claim can be made for representativeness. However, I did find that most Paraguayans had opinions about the two languages and would comment freely and openly whenever the opportunity arose. I spent considerable time in Asunción (five months) studying Guarani as well as collecting data for the historical chapter.

Guarani scholar, Reinaldo Decoud Larrosa.[4] Twenty years ago Decoud Larrosa systematically began to combat the anti-Guarani feeling of some of Asunción upper class. He lectured widely on the value of the Guarani language from a linguistic point of view. He was instrumental in the establishment of the chair of Guarani language at the University in 1944, and has held the chair himself since 1950. He has lectured at schools, in government circles, and on the radio emphasizing the important relationship which obtains between the language and Paraguayan national character. More recently Professor Decoud Larrosa was asked by his government to give a lecture to the President and his senior military officers on "The Influence of Guarani in the Independence of Paraguay". Decoud Larrosa feels that he has been instrumental in helping to turn the negative attitudes of shame toward Guarani imposed by some upper class members into positive ones of pride.

Probably the strongest continuous attack on Guarani occurred during the Argentinian occupation of the country after the Triple Alliance War of 1865-70. At that time, with the influx of Argentinian educators who are said to have been anti-Guarani, the tradition of denigrating Guarani in the school system began. This educational tradition persisted until the present government instituted its pro-Guarani policy and insisted that students using Guarani in the classroom should not be punished.

Guarani remains, however, an object of considerable disdain to some members of the upper class. Therefore, the present government has appointed itself the defender of Guarani. It has supported the activities of the Asociación de Escritores Guaranies (ADEG, Association of Guarani Writers), whose principal purpose has been a *lucha* (fight, campaign) for a wider use of and a new dignity for Guarani. The Ministry of National Defense has made meeting rooms available to ADEG for many of its cultural programs. One of the national radio stations has offered time to ADEG for a daily program in the Guarani language. Such government support of ADEG has stimulated feelings of language loyalty.

ADEG's fight has been a vigorous one. One member told me of his personal intervention in a factory whose owner was not Paraguayan. The owner, who had been invited to the union meetings, tried to insist that Spanish be spoken at these meetings. The ADEG member, however, demanded that Guarani be used since the meeting was for the members' benefit and the employer was only an invited visitor. The owner was forced to acquiesce and the union then offered to provide him with a translator, if desired. Other members cited instances of their defense of Guarani.

For the five years between 1956-1961, the bilingual weekly newspaper *ACA'Ẽ* campaigned for the acceptance of Guarani. This four-page tabloid pointed out inequities between treatment of Guarani and Spanish speakers. It gave full support to the activities of ADEG. It published numerous editorials urging the use and teaching of Guarani in the elementary schools on the grounds that:

---

[4]   Decoud Larrosa is a highly educated person, having been trained not only as Protestant pastor but also as a medical doctor.

– The translation process slows up the learning of basic material (June 13, 1957).
– The prohibition of Guarani in schools prejudices the development of the initially monolingual child and creates feelings of inferiority (June 13, 1957).
– If Guarani were taught well, Paraguayans could speak Spanish better, because they would not confuse the two (March 1, 1958).
– It is the national language and should be spoken and written correctly (April 26, 1958).

The tabloid also urged that Guarani should be taught in the University because:

– Professionals who work in the countryside must know it in order to offer their services (February 21, 1959).
– It is part of the national culture and should be made available to educated citizens (March 1, 1958).

Although some people insist that in the near future Guarani will become extinct, others, probably as a result of the campaign of these agencies, express their confidence that Guarani will continue to grow as long as Paraguay grows as a nation. The President of ADEG[5] feels that Guarani plays too important a role in all aspects of Paraguayan life to die. In his exaggerated view, all true Paraguayans live, love and think in Guarani.

Paraguayans who defend Guarani emphasize the social value of the language. The President of ADEG in an interview equated Guarani with "the heart of the nation", "the symbol of the true soul of the people". Guarani is, in fact, recognized by many as the main unifying force in the country. In the 1960 declaration announcing the new spelling system, the Ministry of War recognized that "Guarani provides a characteristic (typical) seal and a unique physiognomy for the nation" (*Isyry*, 1960, p. 6). Illustrative of the importance of Guarani as a unifying force is the story of the Paraguayan married to a Frenchwoman who remarked after ten years of married life: "... we still do not have any real intimacy between us because she doesn't want to learn Guarani" (*ACA'Ẽ*, May 3, 1958).

In addition to the defense that Guarani is a unifying force, there is the further defense that Guarani distinguishes Paraguay from her neighbors. Leopoldo Benitez justified his translation of the national anthem into Guarani in 1927 by saying that Guarani is "... a current expression of our national soul, a true indication of our Paraguayanism". He insisted that Guarani does not retard the progress of Paraguay but rather serves as a positive force in the spiritual development of the country and helps to assert the unique personality of the nation.

The use of Guarani is also defended on the grounds that it is always more cultured to know two languages than to know only one. This argument is used to counter suggestions that Guarani confuses those who want to learn good Spanish. The

---

[5] The President of ADEG was a man of modest means and one who was definitely not part of Asunción's intellectual élite.

illustrious lawyer Luís de Gaspari in a 1957 speech emphasized the fact that important Paraguayan intellectuals were always bilingual (De Gaspari, 1957).

Those who favor Guarani attribute special linguistic qualities to it. Decoud Larrosa and the self-taught linguist Moises Bertoni both suggested that it has verb tenses unknown in Spanish. Decoud Larrosa stated in a public lecture that Guarani has fourteen indicative tenses while Spanish has only ten. He found that Guarani also has forty six simple modes. Decoud Larrosa felt this fact leads Paraguayans to improve their Spanish by borrowing from Guarani (Public lecture, San Lorenzo, Normal School, August 24, 1960).

Several writers have praised the extensive vocabulary of Guarani particularly in the fields of botany, medicine, and agriculture. Dr. Carlos Gatti's book, 1947, listing Guarani words dealing with medicine is often cited as evidence. Jover Peralta, in his book, *El Guaraní en la Geografía de America*, 1950, demonstrates the importance of the rich vocabulary of Guarani by illustrating the extent to which it has been incorporated into common usage in other Latin American countries.

In response to the criticism that Guarani was merely an aboriginal primitive language, one writer in the May, 1944, issue of the *Revista de Turismo* pointed out that these characteristics did not detract from its linguistic superiority. In defense, as many native speakers do, he pointed to its supposed extraordinary musicalness, its purported apt descriptive mechanisms, and its presumably vital poetic quality. Because of this poetic quality, the author felt Guarani was particularly suitable for the expression of emotion.

Recently, however, another author, Criscollt, *ACA'Ẽ*, May 9, 1957, maintained that Guarani is quite suitable for the expression of abstract ideas as well as of intimate feelings. For him, Guarani is perfectly adequate for the discussion of philosophical, theological, scientific, or other abstract ideas. He argued that Guarani need not be relegated to a single area of human discourse.

The close relationship between Guarani language loyalty and Paraguayan nationalism was reinforced during the Chaco War by the insistence of military authorities that soldiers use only Guarani. This requirement is said to have made for secure communication and united Paraguay against a common enemy.

Language loyalty is also expressed in attacks on those who attack the language. As was indicated, the Paraguayan government has taken up the cause of Guarani and has helped to create feelings of language loyalty, and, hopefully, as a biproduct of this, feelings of loyalty to the country and the incumbent political party.

The tabloid, *ACA'Ẽ*, has led the fight against the anti-Guarani forces. In a 1958 issue of this tabloid, Professor Basilides Britez Fariña declared "... that he who hated Guarani, hated it because he was unfamiliar with its real essence or was incapable of investigating it. In a word, he was a coward, he did not want to accept the national reality" (*ACA'Ẽ*, December 27, 1958).

A frequent line of attack is to call the attacker a foreigner. In *ACA'Ẽ* of April 7, 1958, an editorial criticized those who did not see the need of reading Guarani. Such individuals were called traitors or *gringos*, who wanted to hand the country over to the enemy, and though these people were decreasing in number, they still brought to mind those who favored the abolishment of Guarani after the Triple Alliance War.

Defenders of Guarani also suggest that the opposition is totally incompetent as linguists:

There are certain professors of Spanish who deprecate Guarani without any knowledge of its structure. It is ironic that they do not even know how to speak Spanish. They murder the language of Cervantes. These old-fashioned teachers maintain that the use of Guarani dulls the tongue for other languages, a concept that could originate only in atrophied brains or in retarded minds (*AKA'Ë*, March 3, 1958).

Probably one of the most spirited discussions concerning the value of Guarani took place in print in 1934 between Professor Inocencio Lezcano, a well-known and highly respected teacher and student of Spanish, and Dario Gomez Serrato, one of the most renowned Guarani poets. An outline of the essence of this exchange follows.

On February 14, 1934, *El Liberal* published a letter from Professor Lezcano which objected to a newspaper article suggesting that Guarani be made a regular subject in the school curriculum. He felt that he, like many other Paraguayans, already knew Guarani too well. His knowledge embarrassed him in his contacts with educated people. He saw no merit in the Paraguayan soldier's boast to the Bolivian: "You may beat us in your use of Spanish, but never in the sureness and boldness of our attack." Lezcano also questioned the patriotic value of Guarani.

On February 20, 1934, in a letter to *El Diario* Dario Gomez Serrato expressed amazement that Lezcano was embarrassed by his knowledge of Guarani. Serrato wondered if others found it so strange to speak their native language. He was also astonished that a foreigner proposed the official study of Guarani, while a Paraguayan was scandalized. To him, Guarani represented a source of national strength; it was a language of honey and fire. Additionally, he pointed out that knowledge of Guarani had no bearing on the correct use of Spanish. Serrato proposed the inclusion of Guarani in the regular curriculum.

Lezcano replied on February 25, 1934, in *El Liberal* that Guarani had interfered with his learning of Spanish. He felt that true aristocrats needed Guarani only in speaking to servants or boorish people from rural areas.

This sort of interchange continues today with the proponents glorifying the language and impugning the motives of the opponents. Opposition to Guarani has subsided as the government has continued its fight for Guarani as a symbol of loyalty to country and party.

B. PRIDE

Native speakers normally have an attitude of pride toward their mother tongue. Attitudes of language loyalty are aroused only when a speaker feels that his language has been attacked.

Most Paraguayans are aware of the importance of Spanish in economic, political, and intellectual exchange with the outside world. Some go so far as to consider the use of this language an unavoidable evil. Valdovinos, 1945, in a book lauding the Guarani element in Paraguayan culture recognizes the unavoidable function which Spanish fulfills.

Spanish serves as the vehicle of communication with the exterior. It is instrumental in the formation of the superior culture of the country and in its assimilation with the rest of the world (p. 8).[6]

In general, inhabitants of Asunción tend to be more aware of the value of Spanish than other Paraguayans.

Despite the number of Spanish speakers in Paraguay, very little literature in Spanish has been produced there. A foreign observer commented: "... the Paraguayan himself did not esteem his own literature and often (why not say it?) was not at all aware of it" (Wey, 1951). Pro-hispanists attribute the limited literary production to the lack of a real market for books, a lack occasioned by the size of the country and its poor economy. For the Guarani supporter the explanation lies in the inferiority complex which many bilinguals acquire during their schooling. They are forced to be silent until they can speak Spanish. This, say the critics, creates verbal inhibitions. The effects of bilingualism on Paraguayan literary production are frequently discussed by Paraguayan intellectuals.

Although positive attitudes toward Spanish are prevalent among citizens from the capital, particularly those of the more educated classes, one rarely hears them expressed. This contrasts with other Latin American countries where literary production in Spanish is more highly developed and its expressive values more frequently extolled.

Guarani, however, is often praised as a medium of communication, perhaps because of the attacks against it and because it is the first language of a large number of Paraguayans.

Guarani is considered by its proponents to be very melodious. It is said to be full of onomatopoeia. Cáceres Zorilla in a 1934 grammar of the *Spanish* language cites the following examples of onomatopoeia in Guarani:

ivitú   'the wind'
pararą   'the sound of an empty can'
guarará 'the sound which the rain or falling water makes'
pereré   'to flap one's wings'
pu   'to explode'
pirirí   'the sound of crackling fire'

[6] "Sirve como vehículo de comunicación con el exterior, con el extranjero, como instrumento de formación de la cultura superior del país y de asimilación del resto del mundo." (Translated from: Valdovinos, 1945, p. 8).

pupu   'to boil'
pururú   'noise made by cracking teeth together'
sununú   'loud thunder'

This quality is alleged to make Guarani especially suitable for declarations of love.

From the grammatical point of view, some scholars consider Guarani a perfect language. According to Bertoni, 1936: "Its grammatical structure is simple, its conjugation is regular and unchanging".[7]

Another student of Guarani, Bianchetti, 1944, also commented on this:

Guarani is a perfect language; its morphological structure would fit into those languages called agglutinative-polysynthetic; every syllable, every letter is a descriptive and complete conceptual root and even though preserving this peculiarity, surpasses those modern inflectional languages by the softness, fluidity and sweep of its marvelous turns of phrase.[8]

Guarani is also credited with being more expressive, more profound, and more capable of being abstract, and it is notable for: "... its sweetness and subtlety and for its precise expression of both intimate feelings and abstract ideas."[9]

In addition, Guarani is credited with being an old and elegant language which has made social, historic, and scientific contributions to the New World.[10] Guarani is said to be a vital language because it has persisted in Paraguay in spite of three hundred years of Spanish contact. But such praise could be given any language. Usually speakers are not conscious of the values of their language until they contrast it with another; then, the values of the native tongue are discovered or created. In the case of Guarani praise came from people of all social levels, from both urban and rural areas.

Although literary production in Guarani has never been prolific, the language itself is often cited in conversations as an important part of Paraguayan cultural heritage. In 1945, Valdovinos remarked: "... it is the knot which unites the Paraguay of today with its past."

In the last fifty years Guarani poetry in contrast to Spanish literary production has flourished so that today Paraguayans can point with pride to a literary heritage which is growing and which some people feel has great potential. *ACA'Ẽ* reflected this feeling in its August 27, 1960 editorial:

[7] "Su estructura gramatical es sencilla, la conjugación es regular e invariable" (Bertoni, 1936, p. 9).
[8] "El Guaraní, lo repetimos, es un idioma perfecto; su estructura morfológica cabría apenas entre los idiomas aglutinantes-polisintéticos; pués cada sílaba, cada letra, es una raíz descriptiva y conceptual completa y, aún conservando esa peculiaridad, sobrepasa a los modernos de flexión, por la suavidad, fluidez y vuelo de sus giros maravillosos" (Bianchetti, 1944, p. 19).
[9] "... su dulcura y la sutileza de sus conceptos y la facilidad que ofrece para representar con presición los más íntimos sentimentos y las nociones más abstractas" (Bertoni, 1936, p. 8).
[10] The claim has considerable historical validity. Tupi-Guarani is one of the three major linguistic stocks of aboriginal South America. The language was used as a lingua franca by colonial missionaries throughout the entire eastern half of South America. In addition, Tupi-Guarani speakers were found aboriginally in Bolivia, Brazil, Argentina, Uruguay and Paraguay.

Our present literature in Guarani is limited almost entirely to poetry. ... Despite difficulties much poetry now exists. Our present need is for writers in Guarani to make it a question of honor to produce prose literature. Guarani should live not only in the form of novels but also in works on philosophy and science. ...

Here it is clear that those who are attempting to create language loyalty realize the values of a literary heritage and the need for all types of writing in the vernacular if Guarani is to meet the increasing competition from the more universal language (See: Chapter VI, Stability).

The foregoing comments show that many Paraguayans appreciate the values of Guarani. For forty percent of the people it is their only language (See: *Anuario Estadístico* ..., 1955). Among bilingual speakers, I found people who appreciate Guarani and others who deprecate it. For many Paraguayans there seems to be a continuous conflict which causes ambivalence in their consideration of both languages. Three factors seemed to be responsible for this conflict:

(1) Power shifts between the pro-Spanish and pro-Guarani factions; this shift is particularly noticeable in school policy.

(2) The gap between the monolingual Guarani speakers and the bilingual speakers leads to a confusion of criteria of appropriateness in usage. Although in some situations (formal affairs in Asunción and in rural areas) the appropriate language is well-defined, in most situations the appropriate criteria are muddied by the "mixed" universe in which linguistic interaction occurs.

(3) The importance of Spanish in the outside world is clearly recognized, but *most* Paraguayans have very little to do with the outside world.

In addition to these private factors contributing to positive attitudes toward both Spanish and Guarani, there are several institutional factors which also reinforce these attitudes of linguistic pride. It is thus helpful to examine the amount of emphasis given each language by official institutions.

Spanish is and has always been the official language of the country. All public documents including the constitution are written in Spanish. All street signs and direction signals are in Spanish. Spanish is the language used officially in all public offices although, in rural areas, Guarani is often substituted unofficially. Spanish is the official language of the legislature and the courts. All court cases must be recorded in Spanish even though the actual proceeding is in Guarani. Guarani speakers are at a disadvantage in making contracts. Although Paraguayan law permits official government translators to translate contracts into foreign languages, there is no official translator for Guarani (private conversation with a Paraguayan CPA).

Spanish is the official language of the school system, and, until very recently, it was the only language permitted in the classroom and on the school grounds. Again, unofficially, many teachers found it expedient to use Guarani at the primary level because the students could not understand Spanish. This fact was never reported to the Ministry of Education and no official account was taken of the language problem. At present, Guarani is permitted in the early grades but the earliest possible use of Spanish is urged.

Military personnel are expected to use Spanish on duty. However, frequent code-switching among non-commissioned officers is reported. Almost all basic military instruction is given in Guarani. According to one informant, some army officers insist that Guarani is *the* language of Paraguay. Occasionally, classes in Guarani grammar have been offered at the Military Academy. In 1961, the Minister of Defense at the suggestion of ADEG, referred to the Director of the Military Academy a letter recommending that Guarani again be offered as a subject at the Academy and at the Military High School (Mariscal Samaniego to Alberto Gienno, January 2, 1961).

In all of the churches in Asunción, sermons are given in Spanish. In most of the rural towns, however, there is at least one Sunday mass in which the sermon is given in Guarani. A few priests are renowned for their ability to use Guarani; some people go out of their way to hear these men preach. All of the courses at the Seminary are given in Spanish, although the Seminary has in the past vacillated between complete disapproval of Guarani (prohibiting its use in Seminary buildings), and the inclusion of an occasional course in the language. The religious school for wayward girls has very strict rules about the exclusive use of Spanish and punishes girls who do not obey. However, this school is run by a group of Argentinian nuns who would not appreciate the significance of Guarani in Paraguay. Usually the catechism is taught in Spanish but when a priest makes his rural rounds, it is essential for confessions and sermons that he know Guarani. Catechists in rural areas always teach the catechism in Guarani. In general the Church has been more aware than many other institutions of the monolingual needs of the rural areas; in fact in 1910, Monsignor Bogarin (See: *Nociones ...*, 1910) published a catechism in Guarani.

Spanish language and literature are studied both in schools and by language scholars and literary groups. The Ateneo Paraguayo, Amigos de la Arte, and the magazine *Alcor* have given particular attention to Spanish literature. Scholars vitally interested in Spanish grammar include the following Paraguayans: Delfín Chamorro, Inocencio Lezcano, and José Concepción Ortiz (See: Baez, 1948; Chamorro, 1914; Lezcano, 1946).

Guarani language and literature, on the other hand, have never been taught in the primary schools. For the past few years Guarani has been offered as an elective language in the National High School in Asunción, but it is not offered in other secondary schools. The University has had a chair of the Guarani language only since 1944. Professor Decoud Larrosa, the occupant of this chair, has offered a course in the structure of Guarani for ten years, 1951-1961.

Apart from the educational system, several attempts have been made to organize those interested in studying Guarani language and literature. The first such attempt was made in 1923 when the Cultura Guarani was organized under the auspices of the

Ateneo Paraguayo (*Ortografía* ..., 1940, pp. 15-17). This group of scholars, writers
and government officials stated its goals as:

- The complete study and restoration of the aboriginal language and publica-
  tion of works in it.
- The encouragement of scientific-literary production in this language.
- The gathering of documents relating to the language and to the Guarani race.

To achieve these goals, the society planned to:

- Organize seminars (*seminarios*) in the capital and in the rural areas.
- Stimulate scientific and literary production.
- Unify the spelling and phonetics.
- Establish a library and museum of the race.

Aside from some recommendations in 1939 for a unified spelling which were not
widely adopted, this group does not seem to have accomplished very much in spite
of its extensive program plans.

The Academia de la Lengua y Cultura Guaraní was organized to replace the Cultura Guaraní (*Acta de la Fundación de la Academia* ..., 1942). It was fully endorsed
by the government. In 1944, President Morinigo personally presented diplomas to
new members. This group stated its goals as:

- The compilation of Guarani vocabulary items, presently part of the Spanish
  language, which should be submitted to the Spanish Academy for inclusion
  in the dictionary.
- The identification and removal of Spanish loan words incorporated into
  Guarani.
- The recognition of Guarani as a national language with legal status equal
  to that of Spanish.
- The teaching of Guarani in the school system.

This group does not seem to have been effective either. Although it had a president,
no regular meetings were held, and the group never issued a publication. In 1957
and 1958 (December 28, 1957, May 10, 1958), *ACA'Ẽ* called for the reactivation of
the Academy (even though it never seems to have been very active!).[11]

In contrast to this lack of activity, the Asociación de Escritores Guaranies
(ADEG) founded in 1950, has been extremely active in calling public attention to the
importance of Guarani for Paraguayans. Its principal aims as stated by its president
are:

- The restoration and distribution of native literature.
- The sponsoring of lectures and artistic and cultural festivals.

[11]   In fact, since the death of its president Moises Bertoni in 1963, the Academy has been totally
inactive.

– The elevation of the position of Guarani poets and writers.

– The implementation of a vigorous campaign to win recognition for Guarani as an official language and one with prestige and international validity.

ADEG efforts to achieve these goals include the following:

– Since February, 1960, ADEG has produced a tri-weekly radio program featuring Guarani poetry and native music.

– In collaboration with the Ministry of National Defense it has regularly held free classes in Guarani languages and culture.

– It has sponsored numerous cultural programs in different towns of the interior.

– In 1961, it organized an Exposition of Native Publications calling public attention to the "richness of our national culture".

– In 1960, its members participated actively in the creation of the new orthography which was declared official in that year by the Ministry of National Defense. It also tried unsuccessfully to get other Ministries to accept the orthography as official. In the same year, it sent a letter to the Minister of National Defense requesting the reestablishment of courses in Guarani in the military schools.

ADEG has fought for a proper place for Guarani in the school curriculum. It has urged that Guarani literature be taught at the University level, that Guarani grammar be taught in secondary schools, and that Guarani not be prohibited in the elementary schools. Several members of the ADEG Directive Committee have urged the Academy to play a more important role in shaping the Guarani language. In fact, some feel that the control of Guarani grammar should be completely in the hands of the Academy.

ADEG has been reasonably successful in bringing the importance of Guarani to public attention. The support given by the Ministry of National Defense and *ACA'Ẽ* propaganda are noteworthy in this connection. ADEG has enjoyed its greatest success in Asunción; in other towns it is not well known.

Literary heritage may influence the amount of pride associated with each language. In the following discussion the word "literary" will be extended to include production in all mass media. I found that the amount of pride varied, in part, in relation to the amount, type, and cultural importance of the material produced.

1. *Newspapers, Magazines, Books*

Because the Paraguayan book-buying public is small and book-publishing is a luxury industry, the daily and periodical press is the most important printed medium. In 1960, three full-sized daily papers and a weekly tabloid were published in Asunción.

All of the full-sized papers were written entirely in Spanish. One, *La Patria*, carried a daily two-column article consisting of poems and items of popular interest, written in Guarani.

Although no one is ever taught to read Guarani, the transfer from Spanish is often made and it is considered a real accomplishment to be able to read well. Presumably Paraguayans learn to read Guarani in order to read the tabloids or the magazines.

The bilingual tabloid, *ACA'Ẽ*, probably had the greatest circulation of any paper of this type published to date. Circulation ranged from 10,000 to 15,000 a week.[12] According to the editor, it was written in both languages in order to attract the greatest possible number of readers . The paper was very pro-Guarani, eagerly supporting the activities of ADEG and encouraging the revitalization of the Academy. It was distributed to all of the bigger towns in Paraguay. Occasionally copies found their way to rural areas where they were passed from hand to hand. Here *ACA'Ẽ* was particularly enjoyed because of the reports on crime which, interestingly enough, were reported in Spanish. However, most Paraguayans of a certain education did not consider it worthwhile reading material.

The number of magazines published in Paraguay is limited. None of them is distributed outside Paraguay. In 1960, the most popular regularly-issued magazine was a 10-15 page weekly written in Spanish but entitled *Ñande* (Us, in Guarani). It consistently carried a political cartoon page in Guarani, while local social and political items were in Spanish. Another popular kind of magazine was the song book of current tunes. In all the song books the words appeared in both languages. The oldest and reputedly most popular seemed to be *Ocara Poty Cue-Mi*. These song books were extremely popular among young people everywhere.

Other occasional magazines published collections of poems or short articles in both languages. The Ministry of National Defense published one issue of a bilingual folklore journal, *Yvypyte*, in May, 1960, in an effort to encourage native artists.

Most of the books published in Paraguay have been in Spanish. Exceptions are two or three collections of poetry and a few grammars, dictionaries, and textbooks. *Ñande Ypycuera* (Our Ancestors) a lyric poem, written in Guarani, is the best-known. Individual poems in Guarani appear occasionally in newspapers and small pamphlets. Most of the books in Spanish are textbooks, books on Paraguayan history, and legal texts. Paraguayans have written very few literary works in Spanish.

2. *Radio, Television, Movies*

In the movies and on the radio Spanish is the principal language. There was no television in Paraguay in 1961.[13] Most rural inhabitants had little or no experience with the movies. On the other hand, radios were available almost everywhere and were

---

[12]   The paper had ceased publication by June, 1965.
[13]   Television was inaugurated in September, 1965.

an important means of communication. Radio broadcasts were usually in Spanish. There were, however, the following regular weekly programs in Guarani:

Radio Paraguay
– Daily 15 minute newsbroadcast, sponsored by the U.S. Embassy, initiated in 1960.
– Daily 15 minute class teaching the Guarani language.
Radio Guarani
– Half an hour program twice weekly *Hẹʔẹ tepa ñane ñeʔe* (How sweet our language is!).
Radio Nacionál
– Half an hour program once a week with Professor Decoud Larrosa teaching *pure* Guarani. Program started in 1959.
– Half an hour program once a week giving advice to farmers, *Revista Radial Agropecuaria*.
– Half an hour program twice weekly by comedian José L. Melgarejo.
– Half an hour program three times a week by ADEG. Bilingual with music, poetry, and short lectures.

The other seven stations had no regular programs in Guarani.

In addition to these programs, Guarani songs are interspersed with Spanish throughout the day. Since the government requires that fifty percent of all music played in public be of Paraguayan origin, this means that a fairly high percentage of the music has Guarani lyrics. Many popular songs are written in Guarani and the popularity of these songs abroad has increased their prestige at home.

3. *Letter-Writing*

Virtually all production is in Spanish. Since no one is ever taught to write Guarani (except perhaps in the course at the University) those who need to correspond do so in Spanish. Occasionally, someone writes a letter in Guarani, but this is usually pure exhibitionism.

4. *Advertising*

All written advertising is in Spanish. Occasionally, though, a radio advertisement may be in Guarani, particularly those on programs in which the dialogue is mainly in Guarani.

5. *Plays and other Entertainment*

In the field of entertainment Guarani has a larger place. The Guarani theater has been popular within the country. The outstanding playwright, Julio Correa, wrote and produced approximately twenty plays in Guarani. These concerned topics of local interest such as the problems of the peasant and his household. Some of his work was translated into Spanish. From about 1933 to 1943, Correa had his own company and traveled throughout the country, and even to Argentina, to present his work. When his play "Guerra Aya" appeared in 1933, the Mayor of Asunción wrote Correa to commend him for helping to develop a truly national theater.[14] The newspaper reported that the police had to hold back the crowds who wanted to see the production. No dramatist working in Spanish was as prolific or as popular. Since Correa's death in 1953, his plays have been presented only sporadically and nothing new has appeared by other dramatists.

Between 1925 and 1930 two other dramatists, Francisco Martin Barrios and Felix Fernandez, wrote and produced plays in Guarani.[15] Their work never had the popular appeal of Correa. In the last decade, a Guarani theatrical company was organized and gave several plays in Guarani, but the public showed little interest in these productions. In fact, apart from Correa's work, the dramatic arts have had a very limited development in Paraguay.

6. *Songs*

As mentioned above, considerable indirect support is given songs written in Guarani by the ruling which requires that fifty percent of all music played in public must be written by a Paraguayan.

In summary it may be said that most of the work produced in Guarani is on the popular, folk level. It has occupied a small but significant place in the total artistic production of the country and has appeared principally in popular magazines, tabloid newspapers, poetry, and popular songs.

For residents of rural areas, the radio is the most familiar medium of mass communication with programs featuring music being the most popular. In the urban areas, newspapers and magazines in both languages are popular. The more educated man tends to read in Spanish while the less educated man reads in Guarani. Contact in the rural areas with Spanish mass media is limited to school texts.

As a result of this examination of attitudes of pride toward Spanish and Guarani it may be concluded that:

– Attitudes of pride are associated with both languages.
– Guarani is usually appreciated and supported more by individuals than by institutions.

---

[14]   This letter was in a scrapbook which Correa's wife, Georgina, had put together.
[15]   Fernandez wrote and produced the first play in Guarani *Mboriayjhú pajhá*. It was presented in Asunción on July 6, 1926.

– Spanish is generally the important language of institutions (government, church, school). A favorable shift in government attitude toward Guarani has recently been noted. Guarani plays a larger role in newspapers, magazines, and songs than is played by native languages in other Latin American bilingual situations. Guarani has been supported by several organizations devoted to increasing the status of the language.

C. REJECTION OF THE LANGUAGE

Complete rejection of one's native language almost never occurs except in the case of the bilingual individual or community placing increased emphasis on the usage of the second language. However, in a bilingual community in which one language has greater prestige, the second language may have attitudes of both pride and rejection associated with it. Rejection may be general, denying any value to the language or it may be limited to certain situations in which the language is considered improper.

In Paraguay, Guarani is rejected to some extent but it also is a source of pride. Generalized negative feelings toward Guarani seem to come mainly from upper class individuals whose first language was usually Spanish. Monolingual Guarani speakers, while recognizing the importance of Spanish, seldom reject their native language. When the aboriginal language was rejected, it was on the following grounds:

(1) It is an *atraso* (a step backwards) to speak Guarani because it has no world value from any point of view: economically, politically, or culturally. Spanish, however, is thought to have "modernized" or "civilized" the country.

(2) Guarani is doomed to die despite the nationalistic interests endeavoring to preserve it for their own purposes. Ultimately, it will become extinct because no one is interested in it.

(3) Guarani has linguistic deficiencies. Most frequently mentioned are:

– It is not productive. When new forms are necessary they must be borrowed from Spanish.

– It is not a language but a dialect.

– It has no written grammar.

– It does not have an adequate numbering system.

– It does not lend itself to the expression of abstract concepts.

Some of these linguistic deficiencies have been recognized by Guarani supporters as realistic and attempts are being made to rectify them. Two projects under discussion are the purification of Guarani and the construction of an adequate numbering system (See post: *Awareness of Linguistic Norms*).

Situations in which Guarani is considered improper include the sending of telegrams. One informant reported that in 1931, the telegraph office did not want to accept a telegram written in Guarani. On February 13, 1960, *ACA'Ẽ* reported that a telegram sent in Guarani cost twice as much as one written in Spanish.

In Asunción it has not been considered proper to use Guarani in the schools or in public addresses. Teachers, particularly, are expected to use Spanish. When I requested that a class be conducted in Guarani, the students were usually highly amused. There was a time when the children of upper class Asunción families, particularly the girls, were forbidden to speak Guarani. Government promotion of Guarani seems to have caused Asunción parents to relax their strictness.

D. PRESTIGE

As defined in Chapter I, prestige is the measure of the value of a language in social advance. In Paraguay, Spanish is the prestige language. Although there is a great deal of national pride associated with Guarani, one never learns it in order to advance socially. On the other hand, knowledge of Spanish may help a speaker to better his social status.

In Luque, Spanish has a moderate amount of prestige associated with it. Although knowledge of Spanish is certainly almost always a necessary condition for acceptance into "la sociedad" it is not a sufficient condition. Other factors such as wealth, education, residence, etc. (cf. Chapter III) play an important role, too. Most people who have learned Spanish as a second language have done so in school, thereby acquiring a second attribute of upper class status, that of some degree of education. The combination of knowledge of Spanish and good educational background may be sufficient to raise an individual to the upper class.

Almost everyone *is* interested in learning to speak Spanish, although people living in the rural area seem to consider it less vital to do so than those in town. The desire to learn Spanish does seem to be increasing and more parents are making the financial sacrifice required to send their children to school. In Luque, some parents value a knowledge of Spanish so highly that they do not allow their children to speak Guarani at home, at least in their early years. The same parents, however, will often speak Guarani to each other, thus making it difficult, if not impossible, to enforce their stricture against Guarani.

The moderate prestige value of Spanish is correlated with certain social variables.

The greater the socio-economic differences between the monolingual speakers of languages A and B, the more one language will tend to become the prestige language.

In Luque, only $2\frac{1}{2}\%$ of the population are monolingual speakers of Spanish, and whereas these speakers are mostly in the upper class, a great many more of "la sociedad" are bilingual. This bilingualism permits considerable communication between the two social classes. As indicated in Chapter III, although the extremes of the two social classes are quite clearly defined, the gradation of individuals from top to bottom is continuous and sharp distinctions between the two groups are not made. By contrast, in Peru, the major portion of the upper class speaks only Spanish while a large portion of the lower class speaks only Quechua or Aymara. This cleavage in communication and the sharp class distinctions in Peru makes Spanish one of the more important elements in the definition of social class.[16]

In rural Paraguay, there are no monolingual speakers of Spanish. However, bilingual speakers of Spanish in these areas are not usually so differentiated from a socio-economic point of view as to increase the prestige of Spanish.

The more difficult it is to move from one social class to another, the more significant the association between language and social class will be and the greater the prestige of one of the languages.

I do not have much data on social mobility. However, in view of the continuous gradation of individuals from top to bottom, it is my impression that movement from one social group to another is relatively easy, at least in Luque. A closed aristocracy does not exist in Luque. If one is respectable and belongs to the right clubs one is almost automatically a member of "la sociedad" (This would be impossible in a town like Concepción, but probably not in most others). With this continuous system and a definition of social class determined by many features, movement between classes would appear to be more gradual, less noticeable and less dependent upon a single feature, such as language.

The stronger the ties of one of the languages with an outside community speaking the same language, the greater the prestige of that language.

With the exception of Argentina, Paraguay has been relatively isolated from the other Spanish speaking countries. Most Paraguayan commerce has been with Argentina and pressures for the increased use of Spanish have come mainly from this contact. Paraguayans are embarrassed to speak Guarani in front of Argentinians because they don't like to admit that they speak an Indian language. However, contact with Argentina has been insufficient to really establish a strong association between an upper class and an outside area speaking the same language. In contrast, in Peru, there has been considerable contact with Spain and other Spanish speaking countries; thus the prestige of Spanish is extremely high.

E. AWARENESS OF USAGE NORMS

There are only three occasions in Paraguay in which the appropriate language is rigidly defined. These are: in the rural area, Guarani is expected; in schools and on

---

[16] According to Rowe, 1947, p. 214: "In most of Peru, language is certainly the best single guide to social class, and the language returns (of the 1940 census) probably indicate the socially Indian population with greater exactness than classification by race." Schaedel et al. 1957, p. 7, reports that "... el monolingüismo castellano es ahora una de las tendencias predominantes en el área, tendiendo esto a hacer más difícil la movilidad social de muchos individuos, los cuales hacen un esfuerzo considerable por cambiar su idioma acrecentando así las posibilidades de identificarlas como integrantes de su verdadera clase".

all public formal occasions in Asunción, Spanish is the rule. In all other cases, the choice of language to be used is not as clearcut.

In the rural area, visitors who insist on speaking Spanish are not very highly regarded. The country people say *odzedzapo* or *mostrarse poguasu* (He pretends to be a big shot). If an individual is a resident of a rural area, he must use Guarani all the time or his neighbors will laugh at him and say *odzedzapose*. (He is trying to put on the dog). In the peripheral sections of the town of Luque, this country rule is also applicable even when the individual speaks fluent Spanish.

In schools, Spanish is the only appropriate language. Although at one time, a child who used Guarani in the classroom was called *guarango* (roughly, boor) or given some physical punishment; now teachers limit themselves to encouraging students to use Spanish as much as possible. Teachers in rural schools use some Guarani, but they are usually aware that this is not an acceptable pattern and often persistently deny their need to use the aboriginal language. Most teachers feel that Spanish is the prestige language and a better language and should, therefore, be promoted. It is not usual to hear a teacher say, "It's very ugly to hear a child speaking Guarani", or "Spanish is really our language, not Guarani". On the other hand, other citizens discuss the futility of trying to keep children from speaking their "own" language.

In Asunción, there are numbers of formal occasions where Spanish is expected and this required usage is frequent enough to increase the use of Spanish in informal occasions. For those with considerable schooling, the importance of Spanish has been emphasized with a concomitant "snobbish" rejection of Guarani.

The greatest criticism for misuse was found in these three situations (school, formal situations in Asunción, rural areas). In others, the choice of language was much greater. Criticism for misuse when Guarani was expected usually took the form of ridicule or censure. Criticism for misuse when Spanish was expected usually took the form of correction or censure. The prestige of Spanish did not usually seem to cause awareness of a norm, that is, people did not change languages to appear more cultured. More frequently, awareness seemed to vary with the clarity of cues. The places where the cues were straightforward — in rural areas, in schools, and on formal occasions in Asunción — were found to occasion the greatest number of sanctions.

F. AWARENESS OF LINGUISTIC NORMS

Almost all Paraguayans are aware of the influence of Spanish and Guarani on each other. Most people blame their poor Spanish on Guarani. Many feel that *Guaraní entorpece la lengua* (Guarani dulls the tongue) and as a result, people are unable to speak correct Spanish. Others argue that there is no reason for one language to affect the other, if both languages are property taught. Professor Decoud Larrosa insists that the argument of *entorpecer* is fallacious since many people are able to speak the two languages correctly. Everyone seems to recognize the fact that each language has borrowed from the other. The word *dzopará* (mixture) is often used in referring to the interference phenomena in both languages.

The major discussion and correction of Spanish occurs in the schools. School teachers often remarked on how poorly Spanish is spoken. In general, Paraguayans seem very self-conscious about their use of Spanish and their apparent lack of good orators. Although there is no recognized arbiter of Spanish usage, there are several grammarians who are recognized as experts and who try to insist on certain grammatical forms (Lezcano, Chamorro, Concepción Ortiz).

Many informants assured me that no one spoke good Guarani any longer; the language was always mixed. Often heard was the assertion that older people spoke "purer" Guarani. Judging by the older people with whom I was able to converse, most older people had now adapted to current style and spoke no "purer" Guarani than did younger people. Other people suggested that some scholars and some poets spoke "good" Guarani. Among these, Professor Decoud Larrosa was often mentioned, although for some, it was felt that he had borrowed too much from old Tupi.

Pro-Guarani speakers seemed very interested in purifying and codifying Guarani so that it might be considered legitimate and valuable. The pro-hispanist felt that codification of Guarani is impossible or wasteful. Pro-Guarani informants were aware of the potential importance of the Academy in establishing standard criteria. They seemed to credit the Academy with all the work done by Decoud Larrosa and ADEG. Many knew of Decoud Larrosa's radio program and could discuss the points covered in his most recent broadcast, although usually his recommendations in regard to vocabulary were not followed in practice.

Standards of pronunciation seemed to occupy little or no place in discussions of correct Guarani. Most people did not discuss dialect differences. The only place felt to have distinctive pronunciation was Villarrica, a town known for its unusual intonation patterns.

Probably the most disputed linguistic issue in regard to Guarani has been the establishment of a standard orthography (See: Decoud Larrosa, 1946, for a summary of these disputes). It is felt that in order to prepare textbooks and to teach Guarani properly one orthography should be agreed upon. In many ways, all standardization is equated with the establishment of a single spelling system. Once this is achieved, it will be possible, many feel, to make Guarani official. Discussion of an orthography has consumed much of the energies of the Academy and ADEG. The importance of a standard orthography was an issue fifty years ago when Dr. M. S. Bertoni had his system accepted by Paraguayan writers and philologists (Bertoni, 1914).

In 1940, the Cultura Guaraní published a new system which was not accepted by the public either (*Ortografía de la Lengua Guaraní*, 1940). Once again in 1950, the first Congress of Tupi-Guarani, held in Montevideo, voted for and adopted an alphabet. (See: *Primer Congreso de la Lengua Guaraní*, 1950, for the many articles prepared for this Congress on spelling problems). Professor Decoud Larrosa has used this particular alphabet in his university course ever since. However, other Guarani writers did not accept it and used whatever system with which they were familiar. In 1960, by proclamation of the Ministry of National Defense, a new system was approved (*Ysyry*, May, 1960). This system was completely accepted by ADEG and the Academy but not by Professor Decoud Larrosa and Father Guasch, another Guarani scholar. ADEG and ACA'Ẽ promoted the system and encouraged writers and schools to adopt it. Although discussion continues, a standard spelling has not yet been accepted.

It is interesting to note here a similar vigorous discussion in Peru of the importance of and difficulties in establishing a standard orthography for Quechua and Aymara (*Escritura* ..., 1954, "Alfabeto fonético ...", 1959). This also seems to be the case for Créole in Haiti. The problems were similar: To what extent should the new spelling system use the alphabet of the prestige language (e.g. French and Spanish) or to what extent should the new spelling system be based on an analysis of the phonemic system and a representation thereof of the secondary language? As an example, Paraguayan scholars question whether the voiceless palatal sibilant /š/ should be written with the existing Spanish letters *ch* or should the more common representation of the sound *sh* be used?

Most people, bilingual or monolingual, were aware of the fact that they did not speak "pure" Guarani but rather *dzopará* (mixture). However, the ability to identify non-Guarani items in a Guarani text varied in direct proportion to the amount of Spanish a speaker knew. The more Spanish a speaker knew, the more he was able to identify non-Guarani items in a text. There was, however, no necessary correlation between proficiency and awareness.

Although all Guarani supporters felt that the hybrid language spoken detracted from the value of the pure language, they differed as to how it could be improved. Discussions of changes in Guarani vocabulary seemed to be divided into three types:

– The need for the elimination of Spanish loanwords. Since, as I found, (cf. Appendix I) a normal Guarani text has between 35-40% Spanish loanwords, this constitutes a tremendous undertaking. Some speakers feel that only those items which have a Guarani equivalent should be purged. Others feel that new Guarani equivalents should be created for those technical terms for which only a Spanish word exists. Others argue that this is unnecessary since every language has some borrowings.

– The revival of a number of old words which have fallen into disuse. Although in point of fact most speakers can cite only a very small number of words which have recently become archaic, the feeling is that there are many such. Decoud Larrosa on his weekly radio programs has brought a small list of these to the attention of the public and it is usually these which are cited. Some people felt

that a collection of the vocabulary of the existing Guarani aboriginal groups
should be made in order to add it to the present vocabulary.

– The creation of new words. Most speakers are aware that Guarani has borrowed the Spanish numbering system from the number five on. At the Congress
in 1950, several attempts were made to reconstitute the old system (see: *Primer
Congreso ...*, 1950). No one today accepts this system although some speakers
cite it. Some speakers felt that Guarani had no real mechanism with which
to create new words and must therefore fall into disuse as a language. Guarani
poets argued continuously against this idea.

ADEG, in all its articles, attempts to introduce unknown or forgotten vocabulary
items. Poets often footnoted their poetry indicating the meaning of the new word. In
all, the poets have been the most active in trying to institute vocabulary changes.

The Guarani poet, Pedro Encina Ramos warns, however, that the enthusiasm for
transforming Guarani into a "pure" language should not be permitted to destroy
accepted forms. He felt that:

One should not effect a completely new creation, in the way that some writers and poets
maintain, rejecting tradition, popular usage and the customs which are and will continue
to be the real heart of all the living languages of the world (Pedro Encina Ramos, ACA'Ẽ,
June 4, 1960).

In an essay expressing concern about the problem of orthography and that of vocabulary increment, another author declared a principal of how interference should
operate:

When one incorporates a new word into a language, it is not the recipient language which
should submit itself to the new word, but rather the word to the language (Bartolomé
Melía, *ACA'Ẽ*, July 6, 1959).

This leads to the further conclusion that:

The phonemes of new words which have been incorporated should be represented according
to the spelling norms of Guarani (*ibid.*).

In sum, all Guarani supporters are conscious of the need for some sort of purification
of Guarani vocabulary and of the need for some sort of control of new creations so
that the language can become standardized and worthy of being an official language.
To date, however, no norm has been established for vocabulary, pronunciation, or
grammar.

Many recognize that the lack of a standard grammar makes it difficult to teach
Guarani in the school system and urge the need for the study of the language in order
to systematize it. It is popularly thought that the Guarani spoken today includes
a great deal of Spanish interference on the grammatical level. According to Decoud
Larrosa, today's grammar is the same as that of three hundred years ago; major
changes have taken place only in vocabulary. According to Bertoni, however, a

number of voices have fallen into disuse and are now replaced by hispanicisms.[17] Several attempts have been made at writing grammars of Guarani (Bottignoli, 1940; Bianchetti, 1944; Ortiz Mayans, 1949; Jover Peralta, 1951; Guasch, 1956). These were mentioned by informants occasionally although they were rarely mentioned as works to be consulted.

In summary, I have found a great deal of interest in establishing a codified norm for Guarani. Guarani supporters feel that if a norm is established it can be taught in the schools and serve as a standard for literary production. To date, however, no particular norm has been established for any linguistic aspect, pronunciation, grammar, vocabulary, or spelling, although attempts have been made at standardization. Several grammars and dictionaries of the language do exist (See above). Least disputed have been standards of pronunciation; the greatest disputes have been over spelling.

In regard to Spanish, data on linguistic norms are not available. Many people have accepted the grammars of Chamorro and Lezcano as norms but many others are dissatisfied with them. It is clear that the oft-repeated phrase: "We don't speak Spanish well" implies a norm is important to Spanish speakers even though no uniform one is established.

The frequent discussion of a norm in Guarani is related to my findings of a high degree of language loyalty and pride. Those who desire to preserve Guarani feel that if the language is to survive, it must be codified and normalized.

It can be seen that the language of prestige is not the only language associated with national values and standardization. As shown, Guarani, although not a language of prestige, has associated with it strong attitudes of language loyalty and pride as well as attitudes of rejection. This combination of positive and negative attitudes toward Guarani causes great ambivalence on the part of bilingual speakers.

---

[17] "Hoy se habla mal y se escribe peor. Han caído en desuso infinidades de voces que son sustituídas por hispanismos que no tienen razón de ser, porque destruyen la belleza y la armonía de la lengua y desnaturalizan su estructura" (Bertoni, 1936, p. 8). Bertoni does not cite the voices which he claims have fallen into disuse.

V. ACQUISITION AND PROFICIENCY

The existence of two major languages in Paraguay — Spanish and Guarani — results in speakers with three different linguistic capacities — a speaker may be monolingual in either Spanish or Guarani, or he may be bilingual in both Spanish and Guarani. The bilingual may have either learned both languages simultaneously as an infant or he may have learned them successively with either Spanish or Guarani being the first language.

In order to understand the type of bilingual community which Paraguay has and to understand the importance of bilingualism to the entire community, we will discuss the social variables with which the acquisition and proficiency of both or either language relate. Among the many possible social variables are the following:

Social class	Family
Age	Locale
Sex	National origin
Occupation	School
Religious affiliation	Informal variables
Political affiliation	

By considering acquisition and proficiency in the light of these social variables, we may add to our understanding of the relation of the two languages to the political, economic, and legal structure of the country. An understanding of acquisition and proficiency will also contribute to our ability to predict the direction of linguistic change, if any.

We are concerned here with the most common patterns and means of achieving proficiency and not with individual variation resulting from differential intelligence or special linguistic aptitudes.

In addition to the description of the social variables with which acquisition and proficiency relate, it is important to describe the social conditions under which each language is achieved and which may facilitate or deter learning. Under what conditions is each language learned? Are the conditions formal or informal, forced or voluntary? Is exposure to either language frequent? In which order are the two languages of bilingualism generally learned and to what degree does this relate to linguistic prestige and pride?

A. METHODOLOGICAL CONSIDERATIONS

1. *General*

The data for this chapter is taken principally from the random sample census made of Luque consisting of 299 individuals, five years and above, and from the house to house census made of Itapuami, consisting of 984 individuals, five years and above. Each individual in a household was interviewed, if present at the time of my visit. Additional data are from interviews with teachers and visits to schools in the area. In taking my census, I found that not all of the members of a household were at home and exact details were not obtainable from those members present. When this secondhand information was scanty or questionable, I excluded the individual from my results. Some informants were not sure of the details as to when and where they themselves had learned the second language. The last is to be expected, since in Luque, at least, one is often exposed informally to both languages.

2. *Proficiency*

Collecting data on bilingual proficiency in a large community is difficult. The investigator is faced with several problems:

(1) "... no generally recognized scale exists for measuring accomplishment in language" (Haugen, 1956, p. 75). The construction of such a scale would involve at least consideration of three factors:

(a) The skills one is measuring must first be defined. In speaking of proficiency is one referring to the speaker's ability to speak, read, write, translate, and/or understand aural material?

(b) The aspects of the language (phonological, lexical, or grammatical) which one is measuring must be narrowly defined.

(c) The resulting scale of ability must constitute a reasonable combination of these two factors.

(2) The measurement of bilingual capacity should take into account the speaker's relative proficiency, because, as Weinreich pointed out, not every individual has the same proficiency, even as a monolingual.

(3) The test, while it should cover the above two considerations, should be short enough to administer in the field during an interview, because in dealing with community bilingualism, large groups of people are interviewed. It should usually be administered by the investigator himself to insure that the conditions for testing are equal for all participants.

In my field research, I did not find nor construct a test which met the above requirements or which solved the above-mentioned difficulties. Such a test is extremely difficult to construct and although attempts have begun to be made to do so, none to date seems to fulfill the above requirements. A. Richard Diebold, 1961b, used a translation test consisting of words taken from the Swadesh basic word list to check the bilinguality of the Huave of Mexico. This test, although it satisfies the requirement of time, reveals only one skill — the speaker's ability to translate certain vocabulary items. A second test measuring bilingual dominance was constructed and used by W. E. Lambert, 1955 ("Measurement of the Linguistic Dominance of Bilinguals") in a controlled experiment testing relative ability to respond to word commands. The test measures, however, only a very limited part of the speaker's linguistic skills, namely relative understanding of vocabulary items. More recently, John Carroll, 1959, has contructed a test entitled "Pictorial Auditory Comprehension Test". This test is designed to measure only aural comprehension, not oral production.[1]

My proficiency data was based on subjective observation and judgment of the skill of an informant. I interviewed informants in both languages using a tripartite scale (none, so/so, good) to measure each informant's ability in speaking, understanding, and reading Spanish and Guarani.[2] During an interview I might switch from one language to another observing the reaction of everyone present. In this way, I frequently discovered an incipient bilingual who, although unable to produce any utterances in the second language, might still indicate some understanding. In addition, I collected data by visits to schools where I interviewed children in different grades, checked their bilingual abilities and attended classes to see what percentage of the lesson was grasped and responded to.[3]

Fitting my impressionistic data into Diebold's useful tripartite scale of bilingualism, I established the following categories: (1) coordinate bilingual — only those individuals who both spoke and understood both languages well. I included here persons

---

[1] According to Carroll, the test takes about forty-five minutes to administer. (This period, as Carroll suggests, might be reduced by decreasing the number of items). In addition to the time problem. there are two other problems. The first is that a wide range of linguistic structures is covered with the result that it is impossible to determine what structures or vocabulary are being measured. Secondly, although probably not as great a problem, there is the possible difficulty of picture interpretation. Nonetheless, the test might be used effectively in the field situation.

[2] The author is quite fluent in Spanish, having studied it for six years in both high school and college and has no difficulty in conversing with or in understanding native speakers of Spanish. Her ability in Guarani is less proficient, having acquired it in the field. However, after three months in Paraguay, she had little difficulty in understanding a running conversation and could herself maintain a continued conversation in Guarani after four months in Paraguay.

[3] Another technique which I tried out but which I did not apply was to have different informants listen to a taped conversation in Guarani and list which items they thought were not Guarani. A definite correlation seemed to exist between the ability to recognize interference phenomena and bilingual proficiency. The person most monolingual in the sample, found that the text was "pure" Guarani. The most fluent and best educated of the sample found the greatest number of Spanish items. However, this test has difficulties when used in a normal field situation. It takes quite a bit of time to administer and it is difficult to insist on individual rather than group participation.

who were fluent[4] but who had some "accent" in the second language, as well as individuals who were fluent but who made the standard sort of lexical interference error of loan translation from Guarani into Spanish (for example: "Yo me asuste grande", rather than "Yo me asuste mucho"). (2) subordinate bilinguals — those individuals who were scored "so/so" in speaking (able to speak but not fluently) and were "good" or "so/so" in understanding. (3) incipient bilinguals — those individuals who could not speak one of the languages but who in understanding this second language scored "so/so" or "good". This assignment of data while clearly based on the informant's ability to speak also represents some indication of his ability to understand (a factor which consistutes a strong potential in later bilingual development).

B. RESULTS

1. Over-all

TABLE 1

Percent of Linguistic Proficiency for 984 Itapuami and 299 Luque Speakers 5 years and above (corrected to the nearest tenth).

	Itapuami (N=984)	Luque (N=299)
Monolingual	33.7	4.6*
Incipient	18.8	4.0
Subordinate	27.0	13.3**
Coordinate	20.4	77.9

* Six were monolingual in Spanish.
** For eight Spanish was the dominant language.

Significant differences between the two areas can be seen in the higher percentage of coordinate bilinguals and the lower percentage of monolinguals in Luque and in the higher percentage of monolinguals and the much smaller percentage of coordinate bilinguals in the rural area.

2. Relation to Social Variables

a. Age

As indicated in Chapter I, the age of acquisition has a considerable part to play in the degree of proficiency in, and probably with the attitudes which people have toward,

[4] By fluent is meant the ability to carry on a continuous conversation without hesitating because of morphological or syntactic doubts.

each language. I will use here a fourfold age classification suggested by Haugen, 1956: infancy, childhood, adolescence, and adulthood, to indicate the approximate age of acquisition of each language.

Guarani was the first language learned by the great majority living in the rural area of Itapuami, whereas, Spanish was the first language of only two informants. Both Spanish and Guarani were learned simultaneously as the first language of fourteen informants in Itapuami.

In Itapuami, the greatest number of informants, because of exposure to Spanish in the school system, said they began their bilingual career in childhood. Often this exposure begins late in childhood since many parents ignore the law prescribing seven years as the normal age for school entrance and do not enter their children until their eighth or ninth year. The following reasons were given for non-compliance with the law: (1) The children are needed at home to take care of smaller children, (2) Some parents feel that small children will be at a physical disadvantage at school and should wait until they get a bit bigger, (3) Some feel that small children should be more mature psychologically before they begin school. Although the majority of the rural children had entered by age ten, a small group began as late as their eleventh year. Of those bilinguals who did not attend school, only a small percent had become bilingual as adolescents or as adults.

Guarani was also the first language of a large proportion (approximately 55%) of my sample in the town of Luque. A smaller but still sizable percentage of the sample (approximately 35%) had been exposed in their infancy to both languages simultaneously. The smallest percentage (approximately 10%) had learned Spanish as their first language.

Because the school system also provided the first exposure to Spanish for many people in Luque, childhood bilingualism was the rule. Those for whom Guarani was the second language usually learned it during their childhood and only a small percentage became bilingual during adolescence or adulthood.

As indicated above, most people have their first exposure to a second language in their childhood. As exposure increases through school, work, or home contact, one would expect increased bilingual proficiency. In addition, the number of bilinguals as a whole is increasing because of greater exposure of the younger generations to Spanish. This is due to the increasing number of persons who are able to attend school as well as the increasing number of years they are able to remain in school (See Chapter VI, Stability).

b. *Sex*

As we see in Table 2, in Itapuami, men have a greater bilingual proficiency than women. If we take a total of subordinate and coordinate bilinguals, we find a difference of 20%. The explanation for the difference seems to lie in the greater amount of education for men, and the increased opportunities for exposure through travel, army service, and work experience.

TABLE 2

Rural-Urban Contrast in Proficiency by Sex in Percentages for those ten years of age and above (corrected to nearest tenth).

	Itapuami		Luque	
	Male (N=353)	Female (N=464)	Male (N=112)	Female (N=160)
Monolingual	16.7	26.3	4.4	1.8
Incipient	15.5	26.5	4.4	4.3
Subordinate	40.5	25.8	12.5	12.5
Coordinate	27.3	21.3	78.5	81.2

In the town area, as indicated in Table 2, the difference between male and female bilingual ability does not seem very great. The difference between male and female coordinates is only 2.7%.

We may note that in contrast to the findings of Diebold's study, 1961b, among the Huave where age and sex were the primary determinants of the degree of bilingualism of an individual, in Paraguay bilingualism in towns was limited neither to males nor to adults. In the rural area, bilingualism is more frequently a childhood skill with more men than women having high bilingual proficiency.

Additionally, in the rural area, among the women, it is the younger women who tend to be more bilingual than the older women, due probably to increased school opportunities.

Itapuami Females	(Relative linguistic ability in raw scores.)	
	17-40 (N=229)	41 plus (N=139)
Monolingual	40	64
Incipient	57	43
Subordinate	60	28
Coordinate	72	4

c. *Social Class*

My general experience in Paraguay indicated that upper class informants more frequently tended to learn Spanish first and Guarani second and to be more proficient (at least in the amount of vocabulary) in Spanish; whereas, lower class or rural informants much more frequently tended to learn Guarani first and to be more proficient in it. Since upper class informants have greater access to schooling, they tend to have a more intensive exposure to Spanish. But by no means did all upper class informants learn Spanish first. Many learned Spanish and Guarani simultaneously.

The two informants in Itapuami who had learned Spanish as their first language were both born and educated in the town of Luque and came from higher status homes.

In Luque, informants whose first language was Spanish usually belonged to households generally classed as "la sociedad", some having had this status for at least one or two generations or else they belonged to households in the indeterminate middle but nearer "la sociedad".

In those cases in Luque where simultaneous exposure had occurred, it was often the case that there was a desire for social mobility.

- Often some change in social status had taken place in the household.
- Families presently in the middle range had formerly been poorer or had come from the rural area. While the heads of these households were more comfortable in Guarani, they often spoke Spanish to their offspring and spouses to offer better opportunities to their children.
- In some middle range homes, both languages were used indiscriminately with a great deal of code-switching. My impression was that in middle range homes, in which parents had some degree of education, no particular attempt was made to control language.
- In one upper class household, several members said that in their infancy they had heard the servants use Guarani and has thus been exposed to both languages. I suspect that among most of the upper class this is a frequent pattern so that simultaneous exposure is probably the rule.

d. *Occupation*

Most informants were not exposed to Spanish first through their job. The first exposure was through schooling. However, some did indicate that their knowledge of Spanish or an improvement of it came from their employment. Usually those living in the rural area who sought work worked in Luque or Asunción. Some even sought temporary work in Argentina and were thus exposed to Spanish. Many monolinguals learned Spanish in Argentina during the years immediately following the Revolution of 1947 when they had sought refuge there and had remained for two or three years. Other informants had travelled considerably throughout the country selling straw hats or other dry goods. In this way, they had had considerable exposure to Spanish. Some women travelled regularly to Luque or Asunción to sell vegetables or meats in the streets or in the markets. In this manner they acquired more Spanish. Others said they learned Spanish while in the army stationed in Asunción or through classes in Spanish which were provided for some army divisions.

Some children were exposed to Spanish while living in Luque or Asunción, serving as "mother's helper", "errand boy", or apprentice. They heard Spanish in the household and also learned Spanish because the families usually sent them to school.

For the rural area, as in Diebold's study, 1961b, it is not the occupation which correlates with bilingual ability, but the degree to which the occupation engages the individual in contact with the Spanish speaking town or city. The Paraguayan situation is different from the Huave because in many cases, even though he goes to Luque or Asunción, an individual may avoid using Spanish since so many people are bilingual. When an individual is not a coordinate bilingual he may prefer to use Guarani.

In the case of speakers whose first language was Spanish, occupation played a role only to the extent that it obliged an individual to converse with monolingual Guarani speakers. This, in fact, means that just about anyone in Luque would need Guarani in his occupation. Both the medical doctor and the priest in Luque cited their daily need for Guarani. Housewives also felt the need to converse in Guarani with their maids and the greengrocer vendors.

In sum, while many Guarani speakers learn Spanish because their occupation draws them to town and they may be required to learn Spanish, Spanish speakers in Luque must almost automatically learn some Guarani because their employees or patients, clients, or parishoners are often monolingual Guarani speakers.

e. *Religious Affiliation*

As indicated, in Chapter III, most Paraguayans are Catholic so this variable does not enter into consideration. The only indication of a possible relation between religious affiliation and bilingualism was the case of the family in Itapuami professing to be Seventh Day Adventists. These people made a conscious effort to use Spanish with their children.

f. *Political Affiliation*

I did not feel it appropriate to inquire about the political affiliation of my informants. As a result, no evidence is available to demonstrate a relation between degree of bilingualism and political affiliation. My impression, however, was that it did not seem to be significant.

g. *National Origin*

Informants whose parents had been born in other countries or who had themselves been born abroad always learned either Spanish first or both languages simultaneously. In Itapuami, there were two instances of this type. In both cases both languages were spoken in the home — one informant had a Brazilian mother and the other an Argentinian mother.

In Luque, I found two instances of individuals who had been born abroad or who had foreign parents and who insisted on using Spanish to their offspring, even though they themselves were fluent in Guarani.

h. *School*

For most of my informants in the rural area, the first continuous exposure to Spanish was under the formal conditions of the classroom. Only a very small proportion of those who knew some Spanish had first been exposed to it outside the school system. A large portion of Itapuami had gone to the school in the area, but approximately 25% had gone to Luque or Asunción for their schooling. Of these, a small group walked or rode to Luque daily, but most children were sent to live in the urban area to avoid the long trip. Many parents in their desire to provide an education for their children placed them in the home of a relative, a godparent or a person of means for several years. These children were frequently expected to help around the house and in return might receive some schooling, the amount depending upon the generosity and interest of the family concerned. Children were also sent to town to serve as apprentices. In these instances, they were usually sent to an accelerated evening school.

For those in Luque whose first language was Guarani, continuous exposure to Spanish also came most frequently in school.

Since Guarani is never taught at the primary school level and is only taught in one secondary school in Asunción, it is always learned informally and casually.

The singlemost important factor in making monolingual Guarani speakers bilingual seems to be the number of grades completed. I found a high correlation between the number of school years and the degree of bilingual proficiency.

TABLE 3

Degree of Proficiency* and the Number of School Years Completed for 817 Itapuami speakers, ten years and above (in raw scores).

	None	1	2	3	4	5	6	7plus	Total
				School Years Passed					
Monolingual	143	27	13	2					185
Incipient	45	44	58	23	3				173
Subordinate	12	13	86	102	42	2	2		259
Coordinate	4	5	19	40	51	38	30	13	200

* Degree of proficiency was considered independently of a knowledge of the number of school years.

Several observations can be made from this chart:

(1) A large proportion (77%) of monolingual Guarani speakers had never

passed a single school grade. Almost all (92%) of our monolingual speakers had passed no more than first grade.

(2) Of those whose bilingual ability was considered incipient, the largest proportion (85%) had never gone to school or had passed only the first or second grade.

(3) Of those having subordinate bilingual ability, the largest proportion (88.8%) had passed only the second, third, or fourth grades.

(4) Of those whose bilingual ability was considered coordinate, the largest proportion (86%) had passed the third grade or more in school.

TABLE 4

Degree of Proficiency and Number of School Years Completed for 272 Luque Speakers ten years and above (in raw scores).

| | School Years Passed | | | | | | | | |
	None	1	2	3	4	5	6	7plus	Total
Monolingual	3				1*		1*	3*	8
Incipient	4	6	2						12
Subordinate	5	7	5	10	3	1	1	2	34
Coordinate	5	6	25	31	20	31	49	51	218

* Foreigner, whose only language was Spanish.

Several observations can be made from this chart:

(1) The number of monolinguals does not correlate to school grade passed because in Luque, 5 of the 8 monolinguals were Spanish speakers.

(2) Of those who were incipient bilinguals, the great majority (83.3%) had either not passed a single grade or had passed only the first grade.

(3) Of those who were classified as subordinate bilinguals, a small majority (64.7%) had passed the first, second, or third grade. It is interesting that a larger majority (64.7%) had passed only the first, second, and third grades than had passed the second, third, and fourth grades (52.9%). This differs from the finding for Itapuami where the amount of schooling relates directly to bilingual proficiency.

(4) Of those who were coordinate bilinguals the large percentage (83.4%) had had third grade or above education.

(5) The opportunities for informal exposure to Spanish in Luque are much greater and would tend to make the direct effect of schooling less than in the rural areas where informal exposure to Spanish is much less.

The importance of the school system in the exposure to and acquisition of Spanish leads us to an examination of the methods used to teach Spanish, the motivations for learning which it creates, and the effectiveness of current methodology in teaching the language. Consideration will be given to the extent to which the teachers are conscious of the effectiveness of the methods which they employ.

It is important to recall that over the years the Ministry of Education has ignored the problem posed by trying to teach monolingual Guarani speakers to read, write, and do arithmetic in Spanish without lessons in that language. Teachers are expected to use Spanish as early as possible. All of the teachers interviewed indicated that they had been given no special classes on how to cope with the language problem.

After interviewing school teachers in both areas, I found that although many were aware of the problem created by this monolingualism, most felt that it was not serious and felt that any difficulty encountered was a normal part of teaching. In most rural areas, the teachers were under the illusion that although their students could not speak Spanish, almost all of them could understand it. My classroom visits generally indicated this to be untrue. On occasion, I requested that a class be repeated in Guarani after it had been given in Spanish. The difference in response was appreciable. Most teachers blame the students' inability to speak on lack of desire. Some teachers in Luque, recognizing the difficulty created by the linguistic problem, tried to use more Guarani. Although linguistic problems are usually greater in the rural areas, the urban schools attract many rural students. The first and fourth grades often cause some difficulties, because it is at these two levels that new rural students generally enter urban schools. (One category of rural school has only the first three grades).

Because of the general lack of awareness (Ministry, normal schools, teachers) of the urgency of this problem, the method used to teach Spanish is largely informal and subjective. In the first few grades, many teachers begin by using a certain amount of Spanish and gradually increase the amount during the year. The most frequent technique used to convey the meaning of the Spanish is through translation into Guarani. The teacher says the sentence in Spanish, translates it into Guarani, and then asks the student to repeat in Spanish. Another technique used is memorization of poems and stories in Spanish. For considerable time, the exercises are completely rote for the pupil. In a class observed in the Itapuami school the first grade teacher asked the students:

"¿La escuela de Itapuami es cómo?"
(What is the school of Itapuami like?)

The students showed their lack of understanding by repeating the teacher's question instead of answering it.

"¿La escuela de Itapuami es cómo?"

In another instance a little girl read perfectly a selection of her first grade reader. Upon questioning her, I found that she had understood very little of what she had read. In order to offset the monolinguals' silence in class, the teachers call on the bilingual students much more frequently.

In addition to reliance on the translation-repetition method used in the classroom, some teachers forbid the use of Guarani in the classroom. This procedure, which used to be very common, has been considerably discouraged recently. Teachers have been requested to encourage use of Spanish but not to exercise sanctions against those using Guarani. In some schools, teachers require the use of Spanish during the recreation period. They also attempt to put monolingual and bilingual students together. A third procedure is to encourage the use of Spanish in the homes of students.

Although students often did not understand the Spanish used in the classroom, insistence on Spanish made them conscious of its appropriateness in the schoolroom. So strong was this awareness that when I requested the use of Guarani, both teachers and students broke into laughter.

In general, as might be expected, the linguistic ability and academic preparation of the teachers in Luque were higher than those of the teachers in Itapuami. Of the four teachers in Itapuami, the teacher who had had only seven years of schooling made grammatical and phonological errors in Spanish. Teachers in the rural areas have the additional problem of very little or no student exposure to Spanish outside the school. The result is that rural students are less skilled than their coequals in Luque. Recognizing this, some parents send their children to Luque or Asunción, particularly if they are serious about the children's progress in school.

Frequently students in the rural areas repeat the first two grades several times. Parents seem to accept this as a matter of course explaining that it is good for the child because he learns more. It is my impression that a high percentage of these repetitions is due to a lack of success in teaching Spanish to monolingual Guarani speakers. If greater recognition were given to the student's need to learn Spanish as a foreign language and if more efficient procedures were followed, the number of repetitions would be dramatically reduced.

All school teachers seem to accept Spanish as *the* language of the schoolroom and of all culture. Many teachers are shocked by the thought of introducing Guarani as a subject in school and feel it would be a waste of time. A few would accept it on an almost equal basis with Spanish while emphasizing the greater importance of Spanish as a cultural medium.

i. *Family*

In the rural area, there is no indication that family background affects either acquisition or proficiency. As indicated, for almost all informants acquisition came through schooling. As a result, proficiency was dependent on the amount of schooling an individual had.

In Luque, acquisition of Spanish depended mainly upon social class, national origin, and amount of schooling. Acquisition of Guarani depended on social class, national origin, and the presence of relatives born or raised in rural areas (See j).

Proficiency in Guarani depends upon informal exposure and in some families, Guarani is played down and therefore, the children do not have much opportunity in these cases to speak Guarani at home. For boys, Guarani is then learned in play groups. Upper class girls often do not learn Guarani as well as their brothers in their childhood.

j. *Location*

Bilingual acquisition and proficiency may be correlated as in the study by Barker, 1947, with the neighborhoods of a town or it may find some correlation with rural versus urban areas.

In Paraguay, the rural-urban contrast is extremely relevant in first language acquisition and proficiency. As indicated, in the rural area, Guarani was the first language of the overwhelming majority living in the rural area. In the town of Luque, Guarani was also the first language of a sizable group (55%), but a large group (35%) were exposed simultaneously to both languages and a small group (10%) had been exposed to Spanish first.

Again, while almost everyone (91.2%) in my Luque sample was either a coordinate or a subordinate bilingual, in the rural area, Itapuami, the bilingual proficiency was almost equally divided with 52.5% falling into the monolingual and incipient categories and 47,5% falling into the subordinate and coordinate categories.

In Itapuami, those who had been exposed to both Spanish and Guarani in their infancy, said they had spent some time in the urban area.

- In the case of three informants, their early childhood had been spent in Asunción where most of the population is bilingual.[5]
- The mother of three other informants was born and educated in Asunción and said she was from a "good" family where Spanish was frequently spoken. This woman had married a man of "la gente" from Itapuami. Although he always spoke Guarani to the children, she tried to inject a bit of her "city breeding" into the children's education by speaking Spanish to them.

In the rural area, the relative linguistic isolation of the area, is achieved through inadequate school facilities, lack of informal opportunities to converse in Spanish and through endogamous marriages practices. In Itapuami the majority of unions are between persons from the same rural area. In 177 unions, 146 males and 144 females were from the immediate area. Only 5 men and 4 women were born in Asunción.

---

[5] The national census of 1951 indicated that of persons three years and older in Asunción, 76% were bilingual.

In Luque the order of acquisition is largerly determined by the individual household. The factors of social class and national origin are particularly relevant here. Also relevant are the place of birth of the ascending generation. If birthplace is rural, then the likelihood of either Guarani or simultaneous acquisition is high. If urban, then only social class and national origin are relevant.

> – In two upper class households, the wife had come from a rural area and both languages were used in the household although it is probable that Spanish was used more frequently.
> – In some middle range households where a grandparent who had lived in the rural area most of his life was a permanent resident, he continued to use Guarani while the parents used both languages.
> – In two cases, lower class household heads had been born in Asunción or in larger towns than Luque and, therefore, felt it important to expose their children to both languages. One informant himself had been born in Asunción and he had heard both languages at home.

Living in an urban area is sufficient to guarantee some exposure to both languages and usually sufficient to establish a reasonable degree of bilingualism (see post: informal variables).

In the urban area for those for whom Spanish was the first language, exposure to Guarani came through contact either with servants or through residence in the country. Some informants indicated that they had spent their vacations in rural areas and learned Guarani by speaking to the residents.

For those for whom Guarani was the first language, exposure to Spanish came first from schooling, then from informal variables and lastly from occupational contact.

In rural areas students learn Spanish for purposes of reading and performing simple arithmetic operations. If a person remains in the rural area, he rarely feels any urgency about learning to speak Spanish. Motivation to learn to speak Spanish is greater in Luque. Spanish is often necessary for routine communication with some citizens and is also learned by some to attain greater social status.

Communication is always the motivation for learning Guarani. In some instances Guarani was needed to indicate intimacy with the addressee. It was never learned to achieve greater social status.

k. *Informal Variables*

A number of means of exposure to both languages exists apart from the above-mentioned in Luque. Although continuous exposure came first from schooling for Guarani monolinguals, additional exposure was available through informal means.

In the rural area, little informal opportunity was available to learn Spanish. Informal variables include:

(a) From friends or on the streets of the town. In Luque the opportunity to converse in Spanish informally was frequently due to the pattern of code-switching and that of frequent use of Spanish by upper class persons.

(b) Although not mentioned by informants, the mass media also represented another source of exposure to Spanish. This exposure probably provided some reinforcement of initial learning.

Guarani is never learned under formal circumstances. Informants whose first language was Spanish indicated the following additional opportunities (besides contact with servants or residence in a rural area) which provided exposure to Guarani:

(a) In play groups. When children, particularly boys, play together they often use Guarani. Some informants said they had picked up Guarani in school, usually during recreation periods. The head doctor of the Luque hospital, who had been educated in Asunción, reported that his boyhood companions had ridiculed him into learning some Guarani. Some conversations, particularly ones including jokes, are so much more spicy in Guarani that if one does not want to be the butt of a joke, one learns Guarani in self-defense.

(b) From popular songs. Often people interested in popular songs will pick up Guarani as a biproduct. In learning the words to the songs, many young people also learn considerable Guarani vocabulary, pronunciation, and some grammar.

C. CONCLUSIONS

Of the three possible courses of action in linguistic acquisition—learning Guaran first, learning Spanish first, or learning both simultaneously—I found that in both Luque and Itapuami, learning Guarani first was the most common pattern. In the rural area, this was really the only pattern. In Luque, learning Guarani first was common but some informants learned both languages simultaneously and a few learned Spanish first.

Haugen, 1956, felt that the importance of a language in a bilingual area could be determined by asking: "Who learns whose language?" In Paraguay, while more persons learn Spanish as a second language than learn Guarani, this is generally attributable to the fact that the large percentage of the population learn Guarani at home and Spanish in school as a second language. The learning often occurs only in this formal circumstance and usage is then often limited to formal situations (See: Chapter VII: Usage). In the rural area, those who do not attend school do not usually learn much Spanish. On the other hand, most Paraguayans do learn some Guarani during their life span. It would be almost impossible to reside outside Asunción and not learn Guarani.

In both the rural and urban areas, some bilingual ability is acquired in childhood. In the interior rural areas, opportunity to learn Spanish is greatest during childhood and adolescence (the school years) and diminishes in adulthood. In the towns there are always opportunities to hear both languages.

In general, Spanish is acquired formally in Itapuami and both formally and informally in Luque where social and economic opportunities to use Spanish are greater. The opportunity to hear both languages in Luque is very high. As a result of this high degree and informal manner of exposure, the level of bilingual proficiency is higher in the town than in the rural area where contact with Spanish is on a formal level in schools, and where often the presentation is not very efficacious.

My description of the social variables which relate to acquisition and proficiency have shown the following:

(a) Amount of schooling is the single most important factor in determining Spanish proficiency. In the rural areas, the actual number of years of school is extremely crucial.

(b) Rural citizens tend to have less bilingual proficiency than urban citizens. Their need for Spanish is less than the urban areas. Rural people living in urban areas tend to use both languages.

(c) Occupation does not correlate with acquisition or proficiency directly but the extent to which the occupation leads the individual to interact with monolingual speakers does. It exerts the most pressure in making Spanish speakers learn Guarani.

(d) In the urban area, social class status exerts some influence on which language is learned first. Upper class members tend to learn Spanish first and lower class members learn Guarani first.

(e) In the rural areas, we have seen that men attain higher bilingual proficiency than women. However, younger women seem to be attaining higher proficiency than older women. Bilingualism is usually attained or begun in childhood in both urban and rural areas. In the urban areas no difference between sexes in bilingual ability was found.

(f) Informal variables in urban areas accounted for the principal way in which Guarani was attained by monolingual Spanish speakers.

No important association was found between religious affiliation, political affiliation, or family and language. National origin played a role only in rare instances where the individuals were not Paraguayan.

The analysis of the social variables important in acquisition and proficiency and their relation to the direction of linguistic change will be discussed in Chapter VI: Stability.

Because Guarani is the first language of a large percentage of people in the district studied, the strong attitudes of language pride and loyalty noted in Chapter IV become easier to understand. However, the strong pressures of the school system are largely responsible for the negative or ambivalent attitudes toward Guarani described in Chapter IV. In the rural areas Guarani is really the only important language and despite pressures to the contrary, continues to be so. In the urban areas, a significant number of factors have combined to make both languages equally important (See also Chapter VII: Usage).

VI. STABILITY

If there is intense and prolonged contact of a significant number of the members of two distinct language communities, one of the following situations may be expected: (1) One of the two languages may become dominant; the secondary language may then continue for a long period of time or gradually die out. (2) The two languages may continue on an equal basis. If only one of the languages survives, it will serve all of the communication functions. However, if both survive, in the speech of bilinguals a division of functions may occur. The distribution of these functions may vary from community to community. In some instances, the functions which each language serves may be mutually exclusive, while in others, the languages may overlay in fulfilling some communication functions. The distribution of these functions is subject to change through time.

My analysis of Paraguayan socio-linguistic history (See: Chapter II) seems to indicate a relative equilibrium in the relationship between Spanish and Guarani during the past 300 years. At times, Spanish has achieved great prestige among some of the population and at other times, this prestige has declined. But both Spanish and Guarani have continued in use from the contact period on and there seems to be no indication of the death of either. Later in this chapter we shall consider whether or not this equilibrium is being disturbed. The distribution of communication functions is discussed in Chapter VII: Usage. Because adequate historical data are not available, I have been unable to determine what, if any, major changes have occurred in this distribution.

In studies of the establishment of a stable equilibrium between the two languages in a bilingual community, certain social variables have been isolated as relevant. Changes in the relationship of these social variables, once the equilibrium is established, will change the equilibrium. Usually these studies have been concerned with conditions in a sizable political area, such as the political state or the relation between a political state and a smaller community. The variables isolated are of two types: those internal to this political area and those external.

Internal social conditions usually isolated as important are the following:

(1) The level of literacy in each of the two languages. Friedrich, 1962, pointed out that "... the general level of literacy also determines the acceptance of any language for national purposes", and that "... illiterate masses, whether primitive,

peasant or proletarian, are semantically hindered from playing a full role in the economic, social and political life of a large nation" (p. 549). In his 1959 article on "Diglossia" Ferguson also pointed to the importance of a limited group of literates in maintaining a stable equilibrium in a bilingual situation.

(2) The relation between political, economic, and social power and the languages used. In understanding the readjustment of the linguistic habits of communities in contact consideration must be given to the language of the dominant group. Dominance may be in terms of only one or all of the above-mentioned factors — political, economic, or social. Each study of a bilingual community must consider the dominance position of each of these power factors. At any time a shift in the power structure may affect the importance of a particular group, its language and the kind of equilibrium established.

(3) The degree of geographic and social mobility permitted within the communities. Extensive social and geographic mobility would be expected to produce a higher degree of bilingualism than restricted mobility. If the different monolingual groups are relatively isolated with little mobility, then a low level of bilingualism is to be expected. Any change in the mobility pattern may increase bilingualism.

(4) The amount of social integration within each language group and between the two language groups in contact. The amount of bilingualism in an area in contact will depend in large degree upon the extent to which each group is open to change. In a completely closed group, little bilingualism would be expected. In a relatively open group, eventual death of one language may be a result. Casagrande, 1955, in explaining the decline of the Comanche language, pointed to the lack of an integrated community and constant contact with whites as two of the principal causes. On the other hand, if social integration is required for political reasons, one of the languages may be promoted in order to increase national unity.

(5) The amount and type of communication between the two language groups. This variable is related to number 3. The amount of communication is dependent in large part upon the amount of mobility. However, the kind of bilingual equilibrium which is established will depend upon the amount and the area(s) of interaction.

Once a stable equilibrium between two languages is established upon the basis of a particular combination of the variables cited, a change in any of these variables may be expected to upset the balance and may lead to the enhancement of one of the languages, and perhaps to the eventual death of the other.

One condition external to the bilingual community has been isolated: the amount of contact of either of the languages with an outside community using the same language. All other factors being equal, the greater the contact with an outside community speaking the same language, the greater the dominance of this language, and the greater the percentage of speakers.

A consideration of the Paraguayan situation in this century with reference to the above variables, seems to indicate that some change is taking place in (1) The level of literacy and (2) The relation between the location of political, social, and economic power and languages involved. Geographic mobility may also be slowly increasing. The number of persons literate in Spanish seems to be increasing regularly. However, since these same persons may also have become somewhat literate in Guarani, the language equilibrium may not be decisively affected by this factor. Nonetheless, the emphasis on Spanish is greater and the increase in the number of Spanish speakers seems considerable. If this increase continues, it will have a marked effect on the number of bilingual speakers. The second factor was discussed in Chapter II. The incumbent political party seems interested in establishing group cohesion through greater emphasis on Guarani, whereas the preceding party sought unity through identification with outside communities, most of whom were Spanish speakers. Since the present party has been in power for only the past ten years, no real effect on either the distribution of functions or on the number of speakers can be attributed to this variable. At present, Guarani is used in many more situations than it used to be, but this may be only a temporary phase which may change with the political party. A part of the change in the number of bilinguals may be due to the increased geographic mobility which has come through new road construction and increased transportation facilities. Twenty years ago in Luque, there was only a dirt road to Asunción, traversed mainly by horses and carts or an occasional automobile. Nowadays, there is constant motor traffic on the paved road between the capital and Luque . Whether because of increased schooling or greater geographic mobility, several informants agreed that more people speak Spanish today than twenty years ago.

Measurement of changes in bilingual equilibrium requires the definition of the term bilingual and the resolution of the difficulties of proficiency measurement. In Paraguay, as in many countries, only one reasonably reliable census has ever been made, so that comparative figures for even a crude analysis are not available.

Nonetheless, using a subjective measurement of proficiency (cf. Chapter V: Acquisition and Proficiency), I measured changes in the bilingual character of the community by examination of my synchonic data. A division of the population into different age groups and a comparison of their bilingual ability was used to indicate the degree of equilibrium. This data here refers to the two areas I studied — the rural and the urban.

TABLE 1

Percentages Indicating Bilingual Ability of Informants by Age Groups (Corrected to nearest tenth).

Itapuami (N=817)				
Age Group	Monolingual	Incipient	Subordinate	Coordinate
10-16 (173)	24.8	22.4	31.7	20.8
17-40 (415)	15.6	18.8	34	30.7
41 plus (229)	31.4	26.1	27.9	13.5

Age Group	Monolingual	Incipient	Subordinate	Coordinate
		Luque ($N=272$)		
10-16 (74)	4	4	17.5	74.3
17-40 (132)	1.5	3.7	6.8	87.9
41 plus (66)	4.5	6	18	71.1

The increase in bilingual ability in Itapuami (the rural area) is quite marked if one compares the two age groups 17-40 and 41 plus.

(1) The number of monolinguals has had a 100% reduction.
(2) The number of coordinate bilinguals has increased more than 100%.

A comparison of the total percentage of monolinguals and incipients with that of the total percentage of subordinates and coordinates shows the increase even more clearly.

TABLE 2

Percentages Indicating Bilingual Ability of "Itapuami" Informants by Age Groups (corrected to nearest tenth).

Age Group	Monolingual and Incipient	Subordinate and Coordinate
17-40	34.4	64.7
41 plus	57.5	41.4

It is evident from these figures that in one generation the rural inhabitants of Itapuami have become much more bilingual.

The change in bilingual ability in Luque does not seem as marked, probably because the number of monolinguals at any one time is much smaller. Nonetheless, there has been a 200% decrease in the number of monolinguals and a 20% increase in the number of coordinate bilinguals. A comparison of total percentages of monolinguals and incipients with that of subordinate and coordinate bilinguals reveals a change.

TABLE 3

Percentages Indicating Bilingual Ability of Luque Informants by Age Groups (corrected to nearest tenth).

Age Group	Monolingual and Incipient	Subordinate and Coordinate
17-40	5.2	94.7
41 plus	10.5	89.1

MARKED- AUFFALLEND, PRÄGNANT

This change in Luque does seem to stem in part, at least from the increased schooling among the younger age group in school years passed, as shown by the following table.

TABLE 4

Number of School Years Completed by Age Group for 272 Luque Informants 10 Years and Above (in percentages and corrected to nearest tenth).

| | Grade | | |
Age Group	0, 1, 2	3	4 plus
10-16	31	18.9	49.9
17-40	16.6	9.8	73.3
41 plus	34.8	21.2	43.8

Changes to be observed here are the following:

(1) A significant decrease in the number of informants having passed zero, one, or two grades in the 41 plus group (34.8%) to the 17-40 group (16.6%).

(2) A significant increase in the number of informants having passed the fourth grade and above in the 17-40 group (73.3%) as contrasted with 41 plus group (43.8%).

Another way of measuring change in the linguistic equilibrium is to consider which language is learned first. Thus, when one language predominates in conversations with contemporaries it may be concluded that a language shift is in progress.

In Itapuami, as indicated in Chapter V, Acquisition, most people learned Guarani as their first language. Two people, born and educated in Luque, learned Spanish as their first language. Only fourteen others, out of a sample of 817, had learned both languages simultaneously as their first language. According to this measure of change, no "language shift" or an extremely slow one is taking place in the rural area. Nonetheless, I did find a steady increase in bilingual ability (Cf. Tables 1 and 2). This increase is due to an increased exposure to Spanish in the schools and probable increased contact with the town. This change in bilingual ability is well-known and is recognized in the popular phrase: "La compaña está muy civilizada por ahora" (The countryside is getting much more civilized).

The increase in Itapuami in school years completed is indicated in the following table:

TABLE 5

School Years Completed by Age Group for 817 Itapuami Informants ten years and above (in percentages and corrected to the nearest tenth).

Age Group	Grade		
	0, 1, 2	3	4 *plus*
10-16	59.3	22.5	17.9
17-40	47.8	22.8	29
41 plus	73.9	13.9	12

Significant changes can be observed in some of these figures:

(1) A large percent (73.9%) of the 41 plus age group had only gone through zero, one, or two grades. A much smaller percent (47.8%) in the 17-40 age group had gone through the same grades. The 10-16 age group is not yet significant here because many are still in school.

(2) A greater percent of those in the 17-40 group (29%) had had fourth fourth grade or above education than those in the 41 plus age group (12%). It is notable that a larger percent (17.9%) in the 10-16 group had already passed the fourth grade or better.

Clearly the number of persons exposed to Spanish is increasing in the rural area and will result in a greater number of potential bilinguals.

In Luque a "language shift" does seem to be taking place if we consider the order of language learning. My data on the 66 houses which had both parents and children present, showed the following:

TABLE 6

Language Usage Percentages for 66 Luque Houses (Corrected to nearest tenth).

Spouse to Spouse			Parents to children		
Spanish	(8)	12.2	Spanish	(32)	48
Guarani	(29)	43.9	Guarani	(15)	22
Both	(29)	43.9	Both	(20)	30.3

Clearly more parents use Spanish with their offspring than with each other.

I would like to point out, however, that language may be learned through constant exposure, as well as by direct address. While parents might address their children in Spanish, often purposefully for school orientation, they themselves offered ample exposure to Guarani in their own conversations. In addition, many people reported that while they spoke to their children during their school years in Spanish, they reverted to Guarani when the children reached maturity. Thus the "language shift" was only temporary. Weinreich himself, 1951, indicated two possible means of observing a "language shift": (1) Through changing proportions of mother tongue segments and (2) Through a change from the habitual use of one language to that of another. It would seem that the present pattern of using Spanish in addressing one's children is only a temporary measure and does not indicate a complete shift in habitual usage or in acquisition.

Consideration of the Luque sample and its first language acquisition pattern leads to the conclusion that a language shift is indeed taking place, but that the shift is not from the use of one language to another, but rather, to the use of both. This can be demonstrated graphically:

TABLE 7

First Language Learned for 272 Luque Informants by Age Group (In percentages and corrected to nearest tenth).

Age Group	Spanish	Guarani	Both	Unknown
10-16 (74)	8.1	39.3	54	—
17-40 (132)	12.8	58.3	28	.9
41 plus (66)	7.5	65.1	24.2	3.2

The first language figures were arrived at by consideration of the languages known to be used in the household and consideration of the bilingual ability of the informant. This was necessary because many of the informants did not remember which language they had learned first. According to the figures, those 41 and above (65.1%) had generally learned Guarani as their first language, but this percentage drops as younger age groups are considered. Of those in the 10-16 age group, only 39.3 percent had learned Guarani first. We note that the decrease is paralleled by an increase not in Spanish as the first language learned, but in both languages acquired as first language. This shift would indicate that the town was becoming more bilingual. This shift is not quite as striking as that observed in my consideration of Age Group/Bilingual Ability (cf. Tables 1 and 3). Those who do not learn Spanish at home are frequently exposed to Spanish in their adolescence in school and through daily contacts so that the number of subordinate and coordinate bilinguals is extremely high.

This increase in bilingual ability is reflected in town in a high degree of code-switching (cf. Chapter I). Often, when asked which language they used in a particular situation, informants replied "dzopará" (*mixture*), referring both to switching between phrases and to the closer mixture within phrases. Informants' reports on actual conversations reveal that a large percentage of casual conversations consisted of a balance in the languages used in a single discourse. The change to increased bilingual ability probably also produces a high degree of code-switching. Although

I do not have historical data to document this, it is said that people used to speak more Guarani twenty years ago.

This increase in bilingual ability leads to the question of how far such an increase might go. Can we expect that the entire population of Paraguay will eventually become completely bilingual or is there a maximum level beyond which we can expect one of the languages to begin declining? No nation is completely bilingual. At the present time Paraguay probably has the highest degree of national bilingualism in the world taking into account the factors of total population, use of the same languages, and the same geographical area. An answer to my preceding question would require a consideration of the distribution of usage functions. If the distribution of usage of the two languages is mutually exclusive or partially so, total bilingualism may be possible and might, in fact, continue for whatever time the other variables remain relatively stable. The high degree of bilingualism in Paraguay and its present increase may offer an answer. Certainly the degree of bilingualism achieved thus far is greater than any degree documented and if the rate of increase in bilingualism continues, the answer may be available within this century.

VII. USAGE

The description of Paraguayan bilingualism thus far has pointed to an unusually highly bilingual area with a slowly increasing degree of bilingualism; ambivalent feelings toward Guarani but not toward Spanish; and, in restricted circumstances (the rural areas, schools, and formal public functions in Asunción), rigid patterns of usage. Apart from these circumstances, determinants of usage have not yet been defined. It is the purpose of this chapter to analyze usage behavior where the determinants are not as clearcut and to determine what variables operate in patterning usage.

In the past decade and a half, analysis of the social variables underlying linguistic usage has been considered in several studies which are discussed below.[1] The number of factors isolated in these studies is limited and concordance among the different studies is found. In some cases the variables are simply listed; in others there is an analysis of the interplay of these variables.

In a description of Javanese respect behavior, Geertz, 1960, lists the variables which determine choice of a particular linguistic level but does not indicate which variable takes precedence:

They include not only qualitative characteristics of the speakers — age, sex, kinship relation, occupation, wealth, education, religious commitment, family background — but also more general factors: for instance, the social setting (one would be likely to use a higher level at a wedding than in the street); the content of the conversation (in general, one uses lower levels when speaking of commercial matters, higher ones if speaking of religious or aesthetic matters); the history of social interaction between the speakers (one will tend to speak rather high, if one speaks at all, with someone with whom one has quarreled); the presence of a third person (one tends to speak higher to the same individual if others are listening) (p. 257-8).

Other studies also list the variables without indicating the linguistic behavior which results from the different variables, alone or in combinations.[2]

---

[1]   Two recent studies survey the full range of possible variables operating in the determination of linguistic usage. These are: Susan Ervin-Tripp's "An Analysis of Language, Topic, and Listener", (1964); and Joshua Fishman's "Language Maintenance and Language Shift as a Field of Inquiry" (1964).

[2]   Hasselmo, 1961, in his description of Swedish-American code-switching, attributes switching to: the participants, the topic, and the location.

An important study which not only isolated social variables but also indicated their articulation is that of Brown and Gilman, 1960. In this study, the authors isolated two dimensions, power and solidarity, to explain pronoun usage in European languages. These dimensions referred to the type of relationship which exists between two individuals, a speaker and an addressee. The power relation could be of three types: speaker to an equal addressee, speaker to an inferior addressee, speaker to a superior addressee. The solidarity relationship resulted in two types, the speaker was "solid" with the addressee, or the speaker was not "solid" with the addressee. Because of historical patterns of usage, the pronoun for second person singular "tu" came to have a common definition as a pronoun of condescension or intimacy and the pronoun for second person plural "vous" had the semantic characteristics of respect or formality. As indicated in Table 1, the intersection of these two dimensions leads to two areas in which the dimensions are in conflict. In Column 1, Row 1, the superiority of the addressee demands the use of the pronoun "vous", whereas, the solidarity existing between the speaker and the addressee requires the use of "tu". Equally, a conflict exists in Column 2, Row 3. In their article, the authors indicate how these conflicts are resolved in the various European countries through time.

TABLE 1A

Consideration of the speaker's relation to the addressee and the expected pronoun (After Brown and Gilman, 1960, p. 259).[3]

	Column 1		Column 2	
Row 1	Superior	V	Superior	V
	Solidary	T	Not Solidary	V
Row 2	Equal		Equal	
	Solidary	T	Not Solidary	V
Row 3	Inferior	T	Inferior	T
	Solidary	T	Not Solidary	V

Brown and Ford, 1961, found the two variables defined in Brown and Gilman,

[3] Read as follows: Column 1, Row 1, represents a conflict situation in which the superiority of the addressee demands the use of "vous" whereas, the solidarity existing between the speaker and the addressee demands the use of "tu", e.g., younger sibling to elder brother. Column 1, Row 3, represents an equilibrium situation, "tu" is required by both the dimensions of inferiority and solidarity, e.g., parent to son. Column 2, Row 2, illustrates an equilibrium situation in which the dimension of solidarity alone determines the form of address, e.g., with an acquaintance.

1960, also determined usage in direct address in American English. They renamed these the degree of intimacy and status. Status in the United States, they find, is based on two criteria: age and occupational status. If these two dimensions are in conflict, then occupational status takes priority. Applying these variables to the data, the authors found that in self-reciprocal address, degree of intimacy determined usage; in non-self-reciprocal address, status was the determiner. In moving from a non-self-reciprocal to a self-reciprocal pattern, the authors observed that it is always the person of higher status who initiated the change.

The Brown and Ford analysis is based upon a consideration of the relationship between two persons. In any dyadic relationship, there is always room for and, in fact, expectation of change in usage. Brown and Ford demonstrate how this change operates: In the self-reciprocal pattern, change occurs as intimacy grows from last name reciprocity to first name reciprocity; change also occurs in the progression from non-self-reciprical toward self-reciprocal.

Two other social variables determining linguistic usage are suggested by Stewart, 1962. Each variable consists of a binary opposition, i.e., public-private, formal-informal. Stewart defined the term "public" as impersonal or representative and "private" as personal and non-representative. Since all behavior is representative in some sense, I assume that Stewart meant the actor is consciously representing a particular status relationship. This is observable in statements by high officials who preface a conversation by ;"Speaking for myself alone". Stewart defined formal behavior as prescribed behavior whereas informal behavior was defined as non-prescribed behavior. Again, since all behavior is, in some sense, prescribed, by prescribed Stewart must mean within rigid bounds or with no variation permitted.[4]

The formality-informality opposition which Stewart suggests, may, in some societies, be not a binary opposition but rather be a reflection of a scale of increasing formality.

The literature discussed has suggested several variables which are operable in linguistic choice and some of which are useful in the analysis of Paraguayan bilingualism. These can be grouped as follows:

(1) The relationship between two or more persons involved in conversation. This would be considered from the speaker's point of view and his estimate of the relationship. In this group, we can put Brown and Ford's intimacy and status variables. We can also add sex as a separate variable. Regardless of intimacy or status, members of the opposite sex might with each other use forms different from those used with members of the same sex.

(2) The attributes of either the speaker or the addressee. Here we can list

---

[4]   Other analyses of linguistic usage include those of Barker, 1947, and Ferguson, 1959. Barker, in his thesis on Spanish-English usage in Tucson, Arizona, used dimensions similar to Stewart's. Ferguson described linguistic usage in situations in which only the formal-informal variable was applicable.

class level and origin. Even though great intimacy exists, certain classes
might prefer different reciprocal forms. By "origin" is meant the area a person
comes from — specifically, rural, town, or urban.

(3) The aspects of the situation. Here I would include Stewart's formality-
informality and public-private variables. Another variable might be the location
of the situation, i.e., rural, town, or urban. Still another variable is the degree
of seriousness of the situation. Many informal situations may obviously be
quite serious.

In our study of language behavior in bilingual Paraguay, the above-mentioned social
variables were considered as possible determiners of linguistic behavior. The data
used were responses from individuals to specific questions about their linguistic
behavior (See: Appendix II for the list of questions). In both Luque and Itapuami
these questions were addressed to one bilingual member of each household for which
census data were taken.[5] Additionally, the questionnaire was used in interviews
with the leaders of the town (political, social, and religious) as well as with school
teachers in both rural and town areas. However, this material is not included in the
count of responses to the questionnaire; such responses are used in the discussion
of the variables in pointing to deviations from the norm.

In analyzing the responses to the questionnaire to determine the social variables
underlying language behavior, the procedures of componential analysis (cf. Lounsbury, 1956; Goodenough, 1956) were brought to bear. The results of componential
analysis are terms (or names or labels) and referent(s) to which the terms apply.
Dimensions common to the referent(s) are then isolated. The result is a semantic
set (or domain) in which the terms (i.e., cultural classes) are defined by a set of contrasting dimensions. An important result of componential analysis is that the resulting model is not just a list of important dimensions; it also specifies how the
dimensions which define the terms are articulated. That is to say, it is not only
possible to list the important cultural dimensions but it is also possible to state
how, in what order, the dimensions are to be applied.

In the Paraguayan situation, there are three terms—Spanish, Guarani, and Code-
Switching/Alternate use of both languages. The specific situations (such as: to your
mother when angry) may be said to fill the slot of the referents to which these terms
apply. Dimensions are then derived from the common elements in each situation.
In the application of this technique to bilingual usage in Paraguay certain difficulties
arise. Whereas the use of componential analysis in the study of kinship terminology
leads to a relatively neat dimensional definition, with each term and its referents

[5] Census data were taken for all households in the rural area of Itapuami and for 72 households
in Luque. The Luque households were selected through random sampling. The order of choice
of respondent was as follows: (1) The head of the household if present and if a bilingual;
if not, (2) His spouse if present and if a bilingual; if not, (3) The oldest bilingual offspring present;
if none, (4) The bilingual questionnaire was not administered.

definable in unique combinations of the variables, such was not the case in the bilingual situation. In no situation did all the informants use exactly the same term. Also, situations defined by the same dimensions brought forth different terms.

Thus, the use of componential analysis for Paraguayan sociolinguistics raises certain problems. We feel that these problems can be resolved and indeed allow a wider application of the technique than has usually been made. A comparison of the use of this technique in the analysis of kinship terms or other systems which are labeled by a language (i.e., color, pronouns, illness) with the Paraguayan situation may point to some of the differences:

(1) In kinship analysis what is defined by the dimensions is the referential content of forms. That is to say, the label used applies to a specific clearly defineable referent. In language usage, what is defined by the dimensions is the situational content. This situational content may have many aspects to it and is much more elusive and difficult to define. This difference we feel is similar to that defined by Frake, 1964, p. 199, between "analytic rules of use" versus "explicit rules of use". Results of the first type yield, according to Frake, an independent definition, that is, one does not have to refer back to the culture in order to define the relation between the kin types Mother's Father and Father's Father. The dimensions *generation* and *sex* can be extracted by an examination of the terms themselves. Results of "explicit rules of use" require that definitions of the dimensions must refer back to the "culture's explicit definitions". Thus, the definition of "solidarity" in Brown and Gilman's pronouns is not something inherent in the persons to whom this characteristic may be applied but must be defined in cultural terms. That is to say, there is nothing inherent in the dyad "merchant to customer" which would imply solidarity. One must look to cultural clues to define the dyad as "solid". Such clues are listed by Brown and Gilman for the definition of friendship. In the cultures Brown and Gilman studied, friends are those to whom you would lend your comb, etc. Thus, in Paraguay, when we study the dimensional attributes of situations we are confronted with the need to define these situations in cultural terms. They cannot be defined independently. The process of finding "explicit rules of use" is naturally a much more complex and elusive one.

(2) In kinship analysis the classes each have a linguistic label (such as "uncle" or "punalua") and part of the task of the analyst is to find the members of this class. In the analysis of Paraguayan linguistic behavior, no class names really exist. The actual language used should not be considered the class name because it does not really lead to a single set of referents which can be defined by the same dimensions.

(3) Kinship terms apply to the entire universe to which they are appropriate. Linguistic usage, however, is limited by the fact that some members of the group are proficient in both languages, whereas, others are not. Usage may vary

depending on the expected proficiency, rather than on the social dimensions which might be relevant if all the members of the universe were similar in their linguistic proficiency.

(4) Since the analyses are based on behavioral data taken from the questionnaires, the results show considerable variation. In analyses of behavior some of this variation can be attributed to stylistic manipulation. While the code (cultural system) might define a situation by an ordered set of dimensions, behavioral variation may be due to manipulation of this code for stylistic reasons. Such stylistic variation has been reported by at least two authors who used the technique of componential analysis. One example is Friedrich's fine discussion "Structural Implications of Russian Pronominal Usage" (no date), in the use of the Russian familiar pronoun with a status inferior who is a love object. In this case, the author sees this usage as a device for drawing attention to the importance of the attribute of familiarity over the attribute of status. Again, Goodenough in his "Formal Properties of Status Relationships" (American Anthropological Association Meetings, 1961), pointed to another example of the manipulation of the cultural system. Goodenough listed the usual deference required in certain kin relationships and then demonstrated the purposeful shock value of violating this deference order. That is, individuals may manipulate the cultural system for stylistic purposes. I have some evidence of stylistic manipulation for the Paraguayan situation. One bilingual woman from "la sociedad" reported that when a drunk man approached her she used Spanish (the language of formal behavior) to put him in his place. Another example of manipulation, although rare in the town of Luque, is the use of language to achieve social status. Some upwardly mobile individuals insist on using Spanish in situations where Guarani would be the expected norm. While stylistic variation is one source of the lack of complete concordance in my behavioral data, another important source is the fact that behavior which is based on the cultural system, is always in a state of flux. Everyone does not always respond identically to all questions on usage because some change in behavior and eventually in the cultural system is always present. Thus, while we can isolate a cultural system at any one point in time based on "norms", variation from these norms may be stylistic, but they may also point to a new direction for the existing model. Thus, a comparison of the use of certain dimensions at two different points in time may be indicative of the direction of cultural change. However, in this chapter, I will be concerned with trying to describe the cultural system at one point in time. The results from the questionnaire do not indicate unanimity but I have dealt mainly with normative usage.

(5) In a componential analysis of a semantic domain (set) the definition of any one term (class) consists of the conjunction of some of the dimensions. That is to say, the difference between two classes may consist in the presence

or absence of a particular dimension, but the definition of any one class consists of the conjunction of a series of these dimensions. In the analysis of the Paraguayan situation, dimensions were isolated but the relationship between these dimensions was a hierarchical one. That is to say the application of these dimensions to a particular class of situations operates much like a Guttman scale.[6] The analysis used here is also similar to the operation of a computer which has the following operations in its logic: if a, stop and choose 1; but if not a, then if b, stop and choose 2; but if not b; then ... (continue until a stopping point is reached).

On first analysis, the use of the two languages appeared to pattern much like the pronouns "tu" and "vous" as described by Brown and Gilman and it appeared that usage would be dependent on the participant's status and degree of familiarity. I thought that Spanish would be used with persons with greater power or those with whom one had little solidarity for the same reasons that the Europeans would use the pronoun "vous". Similarly, Guarani would be used with persons of lesser power or those with whom one had high solidarity. The language used with those who were one's power equals would then be determined on the basis of solidarity (Rubin, 1962).

TABLE 1B

(After Brown and Gilman, 1960, p. 259.)

Superior	Spanish	Superior	Spanish
Solidary	Guarani	Not Solidary	Spanish
Equal		Equal	
Solidary	Guarani	Not Solidary	Spanish
Inferior	Guarani	Inferior	Guarani
Solidary	Guarani	Not Solidary	Spanish

Although the Brown and Gilman chart appeared at first to define the usage of Guarani and Spanish in Paraguay, on further consideration the 2×3 matrix seemed to inadequately define the criteria for choice of language.

(1) Between individuals of high solidarity, status was not an important criterion. Usage was defined rather by the location of the discourse or the formality of the occasion.

(2) Between individuals of low solidarity, again status did not really seem to be an important criterion in the choice of language. In the first place, the

[6] Goodenough has used Guttman scaling in his analysis of Truk deference behavior ("Formal Properties of Status Relationships", 1961). However, the chart which we devised to demonstrate this logical procedure is different (Chart 1, post) from the matrix used in such scaling.

self-reciprocal usage between persons of inferior and superior status made me suspect that the model was inadequate and secondly, other factors such as location, first language learned, predicted language proficiency, seemed much more adequately to explain the choice of language and the resulting usage (See analysis of interviews below).

(3) Even though some usage patterns were explained by the model, many of the results of my questionnaire were not consistent and this 2×3 model did not help to clarify these "mixed "results.

The questionnaire used (See Appendix II) defined the situation and asked which language would normally be used. The questionnaire had deficiencies which may have had a bearing on the results. Some of the questions were ambiguous. For example, Number 26 (What language do you use when angry?) does not indicate with whom one is angry. Informants frequently raised this question before answering. Another difficulty was that not everyone could answer all questions. Some people did not have spouses or children; some claimed they never drank or got angry. A third difficulty was that the answer Spanish/Guarani given by informants in some cases was ambiguous. Unfortunately, I did not always pursue whether the informant meant by this response that he would code–switch, or that some other personal factor unspecified in the questionnaire would lead him to use one or the other language but not both on the same occasion. I took this response to mean here a bilingual response and did not clarify this ambiguity except when additional data was available. Thus, while code-switching does occur in Paraguay, I did not isolate the social variables determining its occurrence through the questionnaire. I also doubt that a questionnaire would yield information on this type of usage.

The questionnaire was given to bilinguals in the rural area and in the town area. The results of these interviews follow. A double asterisk indicates responses which are a majority. A majority is a number higher than the sum of the two other possible responses. For example: If 30 persons used Spanish and 2 used Guarani and 5 used both, the Spanish response would be a majority of cases.

Itapuami (number interviewed — 40)

Unambiguous questions	Guarani	Spanish	Both
1. With your spouse daily	28**	0	1
2. With your spouse when angry	27**	0	1
3. With your parents	34**	6	0
4. With your spouse when your children are present	20**	6	2
5. With your sweetheart in the street	9	6	3
6. With your sweetheart making love	8	5	4
7. With your children	19**	11	4

Itapuami (number interviewed — 40)

Unambiguous questions	Guarani	Spanish	Both
8. With your friends drinking tea	28**	0	7
9. With your friends in the streets of Luque	14	9	12
11. With your boss	9	4	7
12. With your employees	0	0	0
14. With the doctor	7	25**	7
15. With the *curandero*	32**	2	2
17. With your servant daily	0	0	0
18. With your grandparents	32**	0	1
19. With your godmother	22**	13	5
20. With the police chief or mayor	13	19	8
22. To confess	15	15	4
23. With the mother of your sweetheart or spouse	27**	2	1
24. With your servant when angry	0	0	0
28. With your schoolteacher	0	37**	3
29. With the authorities in Asunción	4	33**	2
32. In the "country"	40**	0	0
34. With your neighbors	38**	0	2
35. Drinking alcoholic beverages	22**	2	5
36. With your friends in the streets of Asunción	5	25**	6
37. With the bus fare collector	13	22**	5
39. With your siblings	32**	2	5

Ambiguous Questions (ambiguous as to location, intimacy)

	Guarani	Spanish	Both
10. With your "marchante" (term applies to both patron and client)	22**	3	10
13. To make jokes	25**	1	6
16. With an unknown man wearing a suit	7	17	15
21. With a woman wearing a long skirt and smoking a big black cigar	37**	1	2
25. At a dance	11	7	20**
26. When angry	33**	0	6
27. With unfamiliar well-dressed persons	4	24**	11
30. With a bare-foot woman	35**	0	5
31. With a stranger	5	9	18**
33. In town or in Asunción	4	23**	11
38. When you want to say something intimate	22**	6	10

Luque (number interviewed — 66)

Unambiguous Questions	Guarani	Spanish	Both
1. With your spouse daily	16	10	27**
2. With your spouse when angry	28**	8	11
3. With your parents	37**	10	18
4. With your spouse when your children are present	14	22	14
5. With your sweetheart in the street	15	34**	9
6. With your sweetheart making love	13	34**	9
7. With your children	6	34**	18
8. With your friends drinking tea	25	7	23
9. With your friends in the streets of Luque	12	8	9
11. With your boss	8	16**	7
12. With your employees	4	3	7
14. With the doctor	1	56**	8
15. With the *curandero*	43**	0	5
17. With your servant daily	9	3	6
18. With your grandparents	39**	6	6
19. With your godmother	20	28	8
20. With the police chief or mayor	2	55**	9
22. To confess	12	29**	16
23. With the mother of your sweetheart or spouse	28**	5	11
24. With your servant when angry	9**	1	5
28. With your schoolteacher	0	58**	8
29. With the authorities in Asunción	0	56**	6
32. In the "country"	52**	0	12
34. With your neighbors	32**	11	20
35. Drinking alcoholic beverages	13	4	12
36. With your friends in the streets of Asunción	6	29	23
37. With the bus fare collector	25	21	12
39. With your siblings	29	10	21

Ambiguous Questions

	Guarani	Spanish	Both
10. With your "marchante"	35**	3	16
13. To make jokes	38**	2	22
16. With an unknown man wearing a suit	0	40**	12
21. With a woman wearing a long skirt and smoking a big black cigar	52**	1	8
25. At a dance	5	24	31**
26. When angry	30**	9	17
27. With an unfamiliar well-dressed person	0	44**	5

	Guarani	Spanish	Both
30. With a bare-foot woman	32**	0	14
31. With a stranger	0	11**	6
33. In town or in Asunción	0	18	19**
38. When you want to say something intimate	30**	12	16

Analysis

(1) The first and most important variable to be considered in predicting language usage in Paraguay is the *location* of the interaction. If it occurs in the rural area, Guarani is the rule. Indicative of this are the following answers:

– The majority of answers to Question 32 (in the country) was Guarani.
– The majority of the people living in the rural area and speaking to people living there, too, answered Guarani (See questions 1, 2, 3, 4, 7, 8, 15, 18, 19, 23, 34, 35, 39). Exceptions to these answers usually indicated that the person did not live in the rural area.
– The majority of townspeople answered that Guarani was used with a person living in the country. In question 15, the *curandero* usually lives in the rural area and therefore, Gurani is the rule.

The great exception to this rule was the answer "Spanish" to Question 28 (With your schoolteacher). This is due to the extraordinary pressure on students and teachers to use Spanish in the school. Teachers try to insist on the use of Spanish at all times even in rural areas.

As noted earlier, the rural area was the place where the strongest sanctions against use of Spanish were applied and where people were said to be "putting on the dog" if they did use Spanish.

Outside the rural area, the rule is not as clearcut. In the town of Luque, the situation is completely ambiguous and each situation must be considered according to variables other than location. Since much more Spanish is spoken in Luque than in Itapuami the situation requires more choice. When in Asunción (even though the highest number of bilinguals in the country live here) people of Luque feel they should speak Spanish because they consider it the only language of Asunción. One would never be out of place using Spanish in Asunción, but on many occasions in Luque, Guarani would be more appropriate.

The clearest example of this contrast of usage between Luque and Asunción is seen in the following:

The contrasting answers to Question 9 (with one's friends in the streets of Luque) and to Question 36 (with one's friends in the streets of Asunción) shows a clear trend toward greater use of Spanish.

Itapuami Answer

	Guarani	Spanish	Both	Total
9. Luque	14	9	12	35
36. Asunción	5	25	6	37

Luque Answer

	Guarani	Spanish	Both	Total
9. Luque	6	8	9	29
36. Asunción	12	29	23	28

– In the response to Question 33 (at a dance) many informants said that they considered the location of the dance. If in the "country", then Guarani would be in order; if in the town, then both languages would be acceptable; if in Asunción, then Spanish would be expected.

(2) The second variable which is important after the location is known, is the formality-informality of the interaction. Formality as defined by Stewart and modified by me refers to "a limited set of expected behavior" whereas informality refers to "the normal range of permitted behaviors within a group". Formality relates to a number of factors: certain *social identities* (See Goodenough 1961)[7] may require formal behavior; some occasions require formal behavior. The dimension formality-informality seems better defined on a scale than as a single binary opposition. In Paraguay, I expect that Spanish will be required on formal occasions, while choice may be anticipated as one moves toward greater informality. The choice situation may be further determined by other variables or it may be based on more individual decisions.

The number of social identities in Paraguay which appear to place a limitation on expected behavior are the following:

– a doctor-patient relationship
– teacher-student relationship
– authority-ruled relationship
– lawyer-client relationship
– speaker-audience relationhsip
– boss-employee relationship
– priest-parishioner relationship
– sweetheart-sweetheart relationship
– merchant-customer relationship

The results of my questionnaire showed Spanish was used overwhelmingly for the following identities:

---

[7] *Social identity* according to my understanding of Goodenough, 1961, refers to the interrelationship of the two positions in a status situation.

- Question 14 patient-doctor relationship
- Question 28 student-teacher relationship
- Question 29 ruled-authority relationship

However, in the patient-doctor relationship of the *curandero* we have already noted the priority of the dimension of location. Medical doctors do not usually go out or live in rural areas. If they did, they would be expected to use Guarani, if possible.[8]

Again the importance of location is seen in the contrast between the results of Question 29 (With the authorities in Asunción) and Question 20 (With the police chief or mayor). The police chief or mayor is situated in Luque. As we noted, there is greater choice in Luque than in Asunción, where Spanish is predominant.

Initially a sweetheart relationship is formal. Many young men indicated that when they first started courting a young lady they used Spanish. As the courting progressed, the formality seemed to decrease and some young men indicated they used Guarani. Unfortunately Questions 5 and 6 do not reflect the change in behavior required through time and the results are, therefore, not significant.

Question 11, the employee-boss relationship, showed a small majority spoke Spanish in Luque. This relationship is less formal than the doctor-patient one because of the frequent interaction. But since the relationship is a restricted one, the trend is toward Spanish.

The parishioner-priest relationship reflected in Question 22 (to confess) is an extremely formal one. In Luque, a majority uses Spanish. However, results in Itapuami are divided and I do not have an adequate explanation for this.

Some situations are more formal than others. In Paraguay, dances tend to be formal but there are a number of criteria which dictate the degree of formality. If the dance floor is brick, then the dance is more formal than if the floor is packed earth. If the dance takes place in the center of town, it is more formal than if it is held in the suburbs.

Some topics are more formal. In Paraguay, school subjects, legal and business affairs are often discussed in Spanish. There is an obvious relation between these topics and the most formal social identities.

(3) A third dimension bearing on linguistic choice is the degree of intimacy of the speakers. The dimension is relevant only in town or urban informal discourse since rural and formal discourse are fairly clearly defined.

According to Brown and Ford, 1961, certain factors are predisposing to intimacy. These are "shared values (which may be derived from kinship, from identity of occupation, sex, nationality, etc., or from some common fate) and frequent contact" (p. 377).

For most Paraguayans, Guarani is the language of intimacy indicating solidarity or

---

[8] An interview with a medical doctor indicated that he took into consideration the linguistic proficiency of his patient and would, if necessary, use Guarani. Many physicians from Asunción reported that they had to learn Guarani in order to practice effectively.

identity with the addressee, whereas Spanish indicates mere acquaintance. Clearest indication of this is the practice of Paraguayans overseas who tend to use more Guarani with their countrymen even though they may have used more Spanish at home in Paraguay. This seems to indicate that when abroad Paraguayans establish their identity by use of the more unusual and intimate language.[9]

Degree of intimacy may influence a formal social identity. In speaking to an authority or a doctor, in his role as authority or doctor, a friend might use both languages in a conversation although generally Spanish would tend to dominate the conversation.

In social identities which are not highly formal, a shift from formal to informal behavior is more likely. This shift may occur as intimacy progresses. This is demonstrated in the remarks of young men who said they used Spanish when they first started courting (formal situation). As they proceeded in the courtship and intimacy grew (informal situation), many informants said they switched to Guarani. One young man indicated: "It seems as though when we speak Guarani, we are saying something more intimate and something which is sweeter to us."

While Spanish is the language of non-intimacy, linguistic usage in intimate situations depends to some extent on the first language learned. I was told that rural medical students tend to speak Guarani among themselves in Asunción, while students from Asunción tend usually to use Spanish among themselves. Thus intimacy may be expressed by different language usage, depending on the first language learned.

However, the large majority of the population associate intimacy with Guarani. Even at the most formal dances in Luque, male comments about female behavior were always in Guarani.

Luque answers to Questions 16 and 27 (with strangers) indicate that with people with whom one is not intimate, one tends to use Spanish. I often found this to be true, even in the rural areas where upon arrival, the bilingual was shoved forward to greet me in Spanish. I feel that the responses to these questions are not clearly indicative of lack of intimacy because the location of the encounter is not specified.

(4) A fourth dimension which enters into informal town-urban usage is the degree of seriousness of the discourse. In general, jokes are in Guarani in all spheres (Cf. Question 13). Many informants said that jokes were more humorous in Guarani or that Guarani lent itself to the expression of humor.

Angry discourse is usually conducted in the first language acquired. This is clear from the data on Question 2 in Luque (with your spouse when angry). Those whose first language was Guarani felt that "se rete mejor" (one scolds better) in Guarani, whereas those whose first language was Spanish preferred Spanish to indicate the seriousness of the matter. In response to Question 24 (with your servant when angry) I suggest that the majority used Guarani because it was the first language of the

---

[9] Through interviews and other observations here in the United States, I have found that Paraguayans frequently use Guarani among themselves.

addressee and the speaker wanted to impress the addressee on his own terms with the importance of the matter.

Either language is possible among bilinguals in a completely informal situation in Luque. An example is the situation between friends in a moderate atmosphere (not angry or funny). Compare, for example the results of Question 35 (Drinking alcoholic beverages), Question 34 (With your neighbors) and Question 8 (Drinking tea) where the situation is eminently informal. The results are quite divided.

The set of ordered dimensions in the choice of language may be put into a chart which indicates the order of the decisions and the resulting language used. The left side of the chart always results in a resolution of the binary opposition and indicates a clear choice of one particular language (See Chart I on page 109).

In addition to the immediate social setting, certain additional factors tend to influence linguistic usage and cause deviation from expected linguistic behavior.

(1) School pressures. The strongest pressure to use Spanish comes from the schools. Parents are urged to use Spanish with their children at home to provide more practice. Some informants used Spanish with their children until their offspring had passed school age and then they changed to Guarani or bilingual usage.

This pressure is seen by a comparison of the answers to Questions 1, 4, and 7.

Luque

	Guarani	Spanish	Both	Total
1. Spouse	16	10	27	43
4. Spouse, child present	14	22	14	50
7. Children	6	34	18	58

Itapuami

	Guarani	Spanish	Both	Total
1. Spouse	28	0	1	29
4. Spouse, child present	20	6	2	28
7. Children	19	11	4	34

Thus, in Luque, parents tend to use more Spanish and less Guarani in the presence of and in speaking to their children. Even in Itapuami some effort is made to use more Spanish when speaking to children.

(2) Estimate of linguistic proficiency. People often consider the ability of the addressee in choosing between the languages. Indications are:

– Answers to Question 21 (With a woman in a long skirt smoking a big black cigar) were overwhelmingly Guarani. Responses included the additional information that the addressee was probably from the country or was probably

CHART I

Ordered Dimensions in the Choice of Language

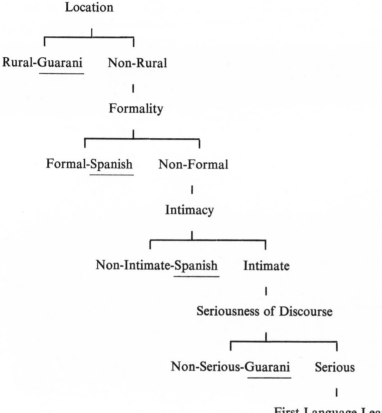

Location

Rural-Guarani   Non-Rural

Formality

Formal-Spanish   Non-Formal

Intimacy

Non-Intimate-Spanish   Intimate

Seriousness of Discourse

Non-Serious-Guarani   Serious

First Language Learned
Predicted Language Proficiency
Relative Sex

monolingual. The predictability of her linguistic ability made the responses unanimously Guarani even though the question did not state this.

– In response to Question 30 (With a bare-foot woman) informants said they thought such a woman might know Guarani better.

– The head doctor of the Luque hospital said that in selecting a language in which to address his patients, he considered which language they might be more comfortable in and tried to encourage them to use it, too.

– The responses to Questions 3, 18, and 23 were, in the majority, Guarani (With your parents, With your grandparents, With the mother of your sweetheart or spouse). This, I feel, is directly attributable to the linguistic ability of the ascending generation. Number 19 (With your Godmother) produced divided responses. Since godparents are usually in the ascending generation and often selected from the more affluent members of the community (also those with greater education and more proficiency in both languages), the divided response is not unexpected. Informants indicated that some godparents lived in the rural area and it was with these that the response was usually Guarani.

(3) Trend toward Bilingualism. As indicated in Chapter VI, Stability, a slow increase in bilingual ability is indicated in Luque. This is also reflected in an increased willingness to use both languages in informal situations. Comparison of data on usage with different generations demonstrates the trend toward frequent alternate use of both languages rather than greater use of Spanish.

Luque		Guarani	Spanish	Both	Total
1. Spouse	G^0	16	10	27	53
39. Siblings	G^0	29	10	21	60
3. Parents	G^1	37	10	18	65
18. Grandparents	G^2	39	6	6	51

(4) First language Acquisition. In Luque there is, in informal situations with friends, some trend to use the first language acquired. This is, at the same time, countered by the pressure toward greater alternate use of both languages. Examples of this trend toward first language usage can be noted in the following responses.

Question 39 (With your siblings)

Language Used		First Language	
Spanish	9	Spanish	4
		Guarani	1
		Both	5
Guarani	29	Spanish	1
		Guarani	26
		Both	2
Both	21	Spanish	4
		Guarani	8
		Both	9
Total	59		

Out of 59 responses, 39 (approximately 66% of the informants) used their first language with their "intimates".

Again in Question 8 (With friends drinking tea) a correlation between first language acquisition and usage is seen.

Language Used	First Language	
Spanish 7	Spanish	2
	Guarani	3
	Both	2
Guarani 25	Spanish	0
	Guarani	20
	Both	5
Both 23	Spanish	6
	Guarani	9
	Both	8
Total 55		

Out of 55 answers, 30 (approximately 54%) used their first language with their "intimates".

(5) Relative Sex. There is a tendency for men whose first language was either Spanish or both, to use more Guarani with other men, but to use Spanish with women who are their intimates. Women ,on the other hand, whose first language was either Spanish or both, tend to use Spanish to both male and female intimates.

In this analysis I have used the social variables determining linguistic usage described by Brown and Ford, 1961, and Stewart, 1962. I considered them in connection with the Paraguayan bilingual situation and tried to describe the factors making a particular language appropriate in a specific situation. The dimensions isolated were: location, formality, intimacy, seriousness of the situation, and relative sex. The dimensions intimacy and relative sex refer to the relationship between the two individuals engaging in a discourse. The seriousness of the occasion and the location refer to the setting. The dimension of formality may refer either to the setting or to the type of social identity between the dyad in a discourse. The dimensions do not combine in an additive fashion to determine usage but rather operate in a priority order.

These dimensions, which are found in any discourse, have been shown to be somewhat skewed by further pressures. Two refer to individual attributes: the estimated linguistic ability of the addressee and the first language acquired by the speaker. The third pressure is that which comes from school orientation.

Finally, the dimensions are skewed by changes in the social situation in the course of time. As more education becomes available and the numbers of bilinguals increase, a trend can be observed toward greater bilingual usage, or fairly unrestricted choice, at least in informal situations.

Linguistic usage in Paraguay reflects the history of Paraguayan cultural contact and settlement. In the administrative center, Asunción, which had the most contact with the outside, there is the greatest use of Spanish. In the more rural areas, which historically had little contact with Asunción or the outside, Guarani is the language

SKEW — SCHIEF

most generally used. Increasing contact with Asunción does not seem to have altered this. Since Spanish has, throughout Paraguayan history, been used for administrative purposes, it is in such formal situations and in discussing related topics that Spanish would be expected and is, in fact, used. Since Paraguay did not develop a sharply defined class system, usage in non-rural, non-formal situations falls back on the equalitarian criteria of intimacy and the seriousness of a situation.

The free variation in usage between the two languages corresponds with the relatively elastic social class structure (cf. Chapter III). As indicated, while the extremes of the social class structure are well marked, there is a continuous gradation between these extremes. In oral discourse, certain situations which might be compared to the extremes in the class structure required a particular language. Between these extremes there existed a series of language choices which did not always reflect exactly the changing social situation. While this free variation does compare with the continuous gradation in the social structure, there is no necessary causal relationship between linguistic usage and class structure. Rather, in both linguistic usage and social class there is a wide area of indeterminancy which in the case of linguistic usage, may be determined by a system of ordered priorities.

This study also indicates that Luque is moving toward a greater degree of bilingualism as reflected in both the increasing bilingual ability of its citizens and the increasing free variation of usage in informal situations. If Luque represents the direction of bilingualism in Paraguay, then we may expect an equilibrium between the two languages to remain so long as the distribution of usage continues to be both mutually exclusive in certain situations and in free variation in others.

VIII. SUMMARY AND CONCLUSIONS

The purpose of this study was a descriptive analysis of a bilingual community to determine the cultural, political, and social factors patterning individual behavior as it related to the two major languages of Paraguay — Spanish and Guarani. The discussion was based upon a representative sample of the population of the District of Luque, Central Department, Paraguay. I analyzed four interdependent characteristics — attitudes (Chapter IV), acquisition and proficiency (Chapter V), stability (Chapter VI), and usage (Chapter VII) — which appear to reflect the cultural, social, and political structure of the area. These characteristics depend upon the history of contact between distinct language communities and upon the subsequent acculturation which is occasioned by this contact (Chapter II). The present socio-economic structure of this community is described in Chapter III.

This study has not discussed two related problems: (1) the effect of bilingualism on the structure of this culture, i.e., the extent to which the degree and type of bilingualism affects the social, political, and economic structure of the communities involved; and (2) the amount of interference in each language which occurs as a result of contact.

Paraguayan bilingualism would appear to be relatively simple. There are only two languages commonly spoken in the country. This area was isolated for three hundred years from effective communication with the rest of the world. The country and its culture are relatively homogeneous. Class structure is in general based upon achieved rather than ascribed status. However, an analysis of attitudes, acquisition and proficiency, stability, and usage indicates a remarkably complex interrelationship between the functioning of the two languages. For none of the four characteristics is there a complementary distribution between Spanish and Guarani.

(1) Everyone esteems Spanish, but is ambivalent in their attitude toward Guarani.

(2) Almost everyone learns some Guarani but acquisition and proficiency in Spanish is dependent on a number of social variables.

(3) There are three areas in which the usage of the two languages is fairly rigidly defined (country, school, and public functions in Asunción). However, all other usage is, in part, defined by social dimensions, in part by social pres-

sures, and in part by individual considerations. Considerable free variation in the choice of language has been found.

(4) While Paraguayan linguistic usage and relative proficiency has been stable for the past four hundred years, in the community studied a change toward greater bilingual ability was seen.

Spanish is the dominant language of Paraguay because it is associated with official use, with the schools and mass means of communication, and with upper class or educated behavior. It is also dominant because it is never rejected as a valuable language. However this dominance is by no means restricted to Spanish. Guarani is also esteemed and loved by a large majority of the population. Guarani is the language of some mass means of communication. Guarani is almost always learned by all Paraguayans, if not as a first language, then as a second language. Guarani continues to be acquired without perceptible decline. And lastly, Guarani is preferred for usage in some situations by most Paraguayans.

Three hypotheses have been formulated and advanced to explain the lack of a strong association between Spanish and attitudes of prestige:

(1) The greater the socio-economic differences between monolingual speakers of languages A and B, the more one language will tend to become, the prestige language.

In Paraguay, and more particularly in Luque, it was found that the number of monolingual speakers was a limited percentage of the community; that the greater part of the community was bilingual and, therefore, a great deal of communication was potentially possible. Additionally, although the extremes between the two classes were clearly defined, the gradation of individuals from top to bottom was continuous and sharp distinctions were not made.

(2) The more difficult it is to move from one social class to another, the more significant the association between language and social class will be and the greater the prestige of one of the languages.

In Luque it was my impression that movement from one social class to another was relatively easy. Language ability, a necessary condition for upper class membership, was not found to be a sufficient condition for upper class membership. This facility in movement and the relative lack of importance given to language in regard to class membership would further explain the lack of the association of attitudes of prestige and Spanish.

(3) The stronger the ties of one of the languages with an outside community speaking the same language the greater the prestige of that language.

With the exception of limited contact with Argentina, Paraguay has been relatively isolated from other Spanish-speaking countries. In the rural areas, although people recognize the importance of Spanish, it is not required for daily communication. Paraguayans who have sought work in Argentina have learned

Spanish, although in the Northern part of Argentina some of the provinces speak Guarani, negating the need to learn Spanish at all.

The acquisition and usage of the two languages has been related to the socio-economic structure of Luque. Of primary importance in both these characteristics is the rural-urban dichotomy. Usage in the rural areas is rigidly defined. In the urban areas there are many alternatives. Acquisition of Guarani is automatically first in the rural area and frequently first in the urban area. Acquisition of Spanish is almost never first in the rural area, while in the urban areas it may be the first language or simultaneously acquired. Much greater bilingualism was found in the urban area.

Both acquisition, proficiency, and usage were greatly affected by formal schooling. In the rural area, acquisition and proficiency in Spanish depend entirely upon the amount of schooling. However, in the urban areas the amount of schooling, while important, is only one of a complex of factors promoting bilingualism.

Age and sex were not found to be extremely important in either acquisition, proficiency, or usage. Only in the rural area was this a consideration — younger rural women were more bilingual than older rural women and rural men were somewhat more bilingual than rural women. In both the rural and the urban area, bilingualism was generally acquired in childhood.

Social class did not enter in usage except insofar as members of the upper class had more education and, therefore, were almost always bilingual and members of the lower class conversely had less education and were more likely to be monolingual. In acquisition and proficiency it was found that members of the upper class more often learned both languages simultaneously or Spanish first while members of the lower classes learned Guarani first.

Variables not directly correlated with social divisions played a considerable role in determining acquisition, proficiency, and usage. Usage was often based upon the degree of proficiency between the speakers, and on the seriousness of the situation.

Acquisition and proficiency in both languages was often achieved through informal contact with speakers of either language or with mass means of communication.

The absence of a rigidly hierarchical socio-economic structure affected acquisition, proficiency, and usage. Neither language is associated with intensive attitudes of prestige ("value in social advance"). Thus, members of the upper class are not inhibited in the acquisition of either language. Acquisition of Spanish by members of other classes is not necessarily based on desires for social mobility. Additionally, because of the lack of prestige associations, free variation in usage is common at all levels of society.

Only in very rigidly defined situations — the rural area, at public functions in Asunción, and in schools — was there an awareness of usage norms. Here strong social sanctions were applied to misusage. These well-defined areas of usage corresponded to the traditional division between administrative usage and the use of the populace. I have found that bilingual proficiency is on the increase in Luque, particularly from

Guarani monolingualism to Guarani-Spanish bilingualism. This increase has resulted in a multiplication of social situations in which the choice of language is dependent on criteria other than those of administration, education, and geography. As a result, there are no social sanctions applied in those situations in which a number of criteria for choice of language is possible.

Historically, while there has been a great deal of communication between the conquerors and the conquered and between class extremes, there has been little contact with other Spanish–speaking communities. Movement within the country has been relatively limited to that between each town and Asunción and not between towns. However, this relative isolation has not produced much regional differentiation and communication between areas is facil when attempted. Recently, communication has been facilitated through the construction of new roads. Bilingual ability is being promoted by increased education and increased support of Guarani by governmental powers.

I have isolated three types of variables operative in choice of language: (1) the relationship between two or more persons engaged in discourse, (2) the personal attributes of either the speaker or the addressee, (3) the attributes of the situation. These combined in the Paraguayan situation in an ordered priority rather than in an unordered fashion. Additionally, certain other social pressures changed the expected udeal results. Pressures were those of school orientation, changing bilingual ability, considerations of predicted addressee proficiency, and finally, a tendency to use the first language learned.

In contrast to the status of aboriginal languages elsewhere in Latin America, Guarani remains an important national language in Paraguay. Attitudes of pride and language loyalty are associated with it and Guarani is freely used in many situations where a European language would be desired elsewhere in Latin America. In contrast to Classical Arabic where Ferguson found complementary usage to be the rule, the situation is much more complex.

Paraguay probably has the highest degree of national bilingualism in the world taking into account total population, use of the same languages, and the same geographical area. According to my Luque data, bilingual proficiency is on the increase. The question which arises is whether we can expect the entire population of Paraguay eventually to become completely bilingual or is there a maximum level beyond which we can expect one of the languages to begin declining? I suggest that all other factors being equal, if the distribution of usage functions of the two languages is mutually exclusive or partially so, it might be possible for a totally bilingual nation to be sustained.

The framework for this discussion of bilingualism in Paraguay may prove useful in the analysis of other bilingual communities. Such an analysis might, in fact, disclose relevant characteristics contributing to the decline of, maintenance or promotion of a bilingual community.

APPENDIX I: LINGUISTIC MATERIALS

A. SPELLING SYSTEM USED FOR GUARANI

The spelling system used in this study is based upon a tentative phonemic analysis of Guarani. The description indicated here refers to the phonemes which are statistically most frequent. The phonemes of Guarani are represented as follows:

Phoneme	Example	Description	Spelling
/p/	(pɨté) 'to suck'	Bilabial, voiceless stop	p
/ᵐb/*	(ᵐbɨté) 'center'	Prenasalized, bilabial voiced stop	mb
/b/	(boteya) 'bottle'	Bilabial, voiced stop	b
/t/	(tɨ) 'pile'	Alveolar, voiceless stop	t
/ⁿd/*	(ⁿde) 'you'	Prenasalized, alveolar, voiced stop	nd
/d/	(do) 'two'	Alveolar, voiceless stop	d
/k/	(kɰ) 'tongue'	Velar, voiceless stop	k
/ⁿg/*	(ⁿgua?ú) 'verbal particle indicating that the action is suspect'	Prenasalized velar, voiced stop	ng
/g/	(guaraní) 'guarani'	Velar, voiced stop	g
/?/	(so?ó) 'meat'	Glottal stop	?
/ʝ/	(ʝasɨ) 'moon'	Palatal, voiced affricate	dz
/s/	(sɨ) 'mother'	Alveolar, voiceless fricative	s
/š/	(še) 'I'	Alveo-palatal, voiceless fricative	sh
/h/	(hɰ) 'black'	Glottal fricative	h
/f/	(aforsá) 'I forced'	Labio-dental, voiceless fricative	f
/v/	(hovɨ) 'blue'	Labio-dental, voiced fricative	v
/m/	(ména) 'husband'	Bilabial, voiced nasal	m
/n/	(aní) 'don't'	Alveolar, voiced nasal	n

* Unresolved as to whether this has phonemic status.

/ñ/	(ñandɨ) 'grease'	Alveo-palatal, voiced nasal	ñ
/ŋ/	(apiŋguá) 'nose'	Velar, voiced nasal	ŋ
/l/	(limasutí) 'lemon'	Alveolar, voiced lateral	l
/ř/	(ro) 'bitter'	Alveolar, voiced flap	r
/y/	(kapíya) 'town'	High front palatal	y
/i/	(iporá̧) 'good'	High front vowel	i
/e/	(ména) 'husband'	Mid front vowel	e
/ɨ/	(ɨ) 'water'	High central vowel	ɨ
/a/	(añó) 'alone'	Low central vowel	a
/u/	(umí) 'those'	High back vowel	u
/o/	(ro) 'bitter'	Mid back vowel	o
/į/	(peteį) 'one'	High front nasal vowel	į
/ę/	(ko?ę́ro) 'tomorrow'	Mid front nasal vowel	ę
/ɨ̨/	(ɨ̨) 'without'	High central nasal vowel	ɨ̨
/a̧/	(tupá̧) 'God'	Low central nasal vowel	a̧
/ṳ/	(kṳ) 'tongue'	High back nasal vowel	ṳ
/o̧/	(moko̧i) 'two'	Mid back nasal vowel	o̧

B. MORPHEME LIST FREQUENCY OF SPANISH INTERFERENCE IN SIX GUARANI TEXTS

The most frequent type of morphological interference in Guarani from Spanish takes the shape of loan words incorporated into Guarani texts.[1] The percentage of words incorporated varies greatly from text to text, seemingly according to the bilingual proficiency of the speakers, the frequency with which they use Guarani, and which of the two languages was learned first. The kind of interference occurring in Guarani differs from that which occurs in Paraguayan Spanish. In Paraguayan Spanish (see post) interference from Guarani most frequently takes the shape of loan translation.

A total of six tape recorded texts was tabulated to ascertain the number of items which were of Spanish origin. The participants in the discourses had the following social attributes:

Text 1. All participants were coordinate bilinguals, most had sixth grade education or above, most had upper class status. Number of participants was 8. Location of conversation — Itapuami.

Text 2. All participants were coordinate bilinguals, most had third grade

[1] For studies dealing with Spanish interference in Guarani see: Cardogan, 1948; Gonzalez, 1950; Morinigo, 1931, 1959.

education, all had lower class status. Number of participants was 3. Location of conversation — Asunción.

Text 3. All participants were coordinate bilinguals, most had sixth grade education, all had lower class status. Number of participants was 5. Location of conversation — Luque.

Text 4. All participants were coordinate bilinguals, all had sixth grade education or above, all had upper class status. Number of participants was 2. Participants were trying to speak "pure" Guarani. Location of conversation — Luque.

Text 5. All participants were coordinate bilinguals, all had sixth grade education or above, one had upper class status, one had middle class status. Number of participants was 2. Location of conversation — Luque.

Text 6. One participant was a coordinate bilingual, one a monolingual. One had sixth grade education, the other none. One was lower class, the other middle. Number of participants was 2. Location of conversation — Luque.

List Number of Morphemes in Each Text

Total number of morphemes occurring in all six texts	—1414
Number of morphemes occurring in Text 1	— 868
Number of morphemes occurring in Text 2	— 424
Number of morphemes occurring in Text 3	— 316
Number of morphemes occurring in Text 4	— 405
Number of morphemes occurring in Text 5	— 328
Number of morphemes occurring in Text 6	— 444

List Frequency of Spanish Loan Words in Each Text

Text 1.	45%	Text 4	32%
Text 2.	37%	Text 5	30%
Text 3.	35%	Text 6	28%

The high percentage of Spanish loan words found in these texts contrasts with the 5 loan words found in the Swadesh word list for Guarani (See post).

C. GUARANI INTERFERENCE PHENOMENA IN SPANISH

Although I did not specifically investigate Guarani interference phenomena in the Spanish of Paraguay, it is apparent that interference often takes the form of loan translation. This contrasts strongly with Spanish interference in Guarani where Spanish lexical items are usually incorporated into Guarani.

Following are some examples of loan translation from Guarani into Spanish which were common in Paraguay. The Guarani model is given first along with its English gloss. Then the Paraguayan Spanish example is given with the closest Standard Spanish form.

Guarani Model and English Gloss

Paraguayan Spanish Based on Guarani Model, Standard Spanish Form, English Gloss

edzu*mína*.
    (edzú "come", imperative form;
    -mína "a little," in an endearing tone)
    (*Please* come.)

veni *un poco*.
    Std. Spanish: venga *por favor*.
    (veni "come," imperative form;
    un poco "a little," referring to
    quantity, not time; por favor "please.")
    Note: mína ≅ un poco.

tuisha iterei añemondíi.
    (tuisha "big," in time and size;
    iterei 'an intensifier;'
    añemondíi " I was frightened.")
    (I was *very* frightened.)

yo me asusté *tan grande*.
    Std. Spanish: yo me asusté *mucho*.
    (yo me asusté "I was frightened;"
    tan "so", an intensifier;
    grande "big" in size;
    mucho "a lot.")
    Note: tuisha iterei ≅ tan grande.

eguahẹmíke.
    (eguahẹ "come in, arrive," imperative form;
    -mi "a little" in an endearing tone;
    -ke imperative form)
    (Won't you *come in?*)

¿no vas a *llegar*?
    Std. Spanish: ¿ No vas a *entrar*?
    (no vas a "aren't you going to ...?"
    llegar "arrive;"
    entrar "enter.")
    Note: -guahẹ ≅ llegar.

añe?e *vaí vaí*.
(añe?e "I speak;"
    vaí "bad, badly;"
    vaí vaí "very badly")
    (I speak poorly).

yo hablo *mal mal*.
    Std. Spanish: Yo hablo *mas o menos*.
    or Yo hablo mal.
    (yo hablo "I speak;"
    mal "bad, badly;"
    mas o menos "more or less.")
    Note: Guarani iteration is transferred to Spanish where it is not used.

pe *añenandu haguepe*.
    (pe "that;"

el lugar en que *me sentí*.
    Std. Spanish: El lugar en donde *nací*.

Guarani Model and English Gloss

Paraguayan Spanish Based on Guarani Model, Standard Spanish From, English Gloss

añenandu hague- "place where I was born;"
-pe "in which;"
-nandu "be born, feel (something)")
(The place where I was born.)

(el lugar "the place;"
en que "in which"
sentirse "to feel oneself, to feel;"
en donde "in which, where;"
nacer "to be born.")
Note: añenandu hague ≅ me sentí.

nde rendape adzú.
(nde "your;"
renda- "side, place;"
-pe "to your;"
adzú "I come;")
(I come to visit you.)

me fuí *junto a usted.*
Std. Spanish: Me fuí *a su casa.*
(me fuí "I went;"
junto a "near, next to;"
usted "you;"
a su casa "to your house.")
Note: nde rendape ≅ junto a usted.

koẹro *ramo* haʔe oúta.
(koẹro "tomorrow;"
ramo "only, to have just done something;"
haʔe "he;"
oúta "will come (3 pers sg.);")
(It will be tomorrow before he comes.)

recién mañana vendrá.
Std. Spanish: *Solamente* mañana vendrá.
(recién "just, to have just done something;"
mañana "tomorrow;"
vendrá "he will come;"
solamente "only.")
Note: ramo ≅ recién.

she *rasá mombiri.*
(she "me, I;"
rasá "he passes, passed;"
mombiri "far away;")
(I was beaten by a mile.)

me *ganó lejos.*
Std. Spanish: Me ganó *por mucho.*
(me "me;"
ganó "he won;"
lejos "far away;"
por mucho "a great deal.")
Note: Guarani idiom, rasá mombiri ≅ ganar lejos.

haʔe kuera opuka*pá*ta ñande *rehe.*
(haʔe kuera "they;"
opuka "laugh (3rd pers. sg.);"
-pa- "totally, completely;"
-ta "future tense;"

se va reír *todo por* nosotro.
Std. Spanish: Se va reir *de* nosotros *mucho.*
(se va reír "they will laugh;"
todo "all;"

Guarani Model and English Gloss	*Paraguayan Spanish Based on Guarani Model, Standard Spanish Form, English Gloss*
ñande "us;" rehe "at;") (They will laugh at us a lot.)	por "by, for;" de "at"; mucho "a lot.") Note: -pa ≅ todo; rehe ≅ por.
adzupi peteị iviraraká*me*. (adzupi "I climb;" peteị "one, a;" iviraraką "tree;" -me "in;") (I climb a tree.)	subo *por* un arbol. Std. Spanish: Subo un arbol. (subo "I climb;" por "by, through;" un arbol "a tree.") Note: Since Guarani uses a preposition with "to climb" this is translated incorrectly into Spanish and produces the non-Standard form "subir por."

D. SWADESH 100 WORD LIST IN GUARANI, SPANISH, AND ENGLISH

(Guarani elicited by giving the Spanish word. Spanish after Diebold, 1961.)

Guarani	*Spanish*	*English*
she	yo	I
nde	tu	thou
ñande, oré	nosotros	we
péva, kóva	este	this
amóa	aquel	that
maa, maava	quien	who
mbaé	que	what
nahániri	no	no
*entéro, enterovéva	todos	all
hetá	muchos	many
dzaguá	perro	dog
ki	piojo	louse
iviramáta	arbol	tree
haị	semilla	seed
hogué	hoja	leaf

* Spanish loan words

Guarani	Spanish	English
peteĩ	uno	one
mokọi	dos	two
tuishá	grande	big
pukú	largo	long
mishĩ	chico	small
kuñá	mujer	woman
kuimbaé	hombre	man
*hente	gente	person (human being)
pirá	pez	fish
guɨrá	pájaro	bird
hapó	raíz	root
iviɨrapiré	corteza	bark
piré	piel	skin
so?ó	carne	meat (flesh)
huguɨ	sangre	blood
kangué	hueso	bone
ñandɨ	grasa	fat (grease)
rupi?á	huevo	egg
hatĩ	cuerno	horn
huguai	cola	tail
tĩ	nariz	nose
dzurú	boca	mouth
haɨ	diente	tooth
kụ	lengua	tongue
pɨapé	garra	claw
káma	senos	breast
*kọrasọ́	corazón	heart
pɨ?á	higado	liver
hoi?ú	bebe	drink
okarú	come	eat
hei?ĩ	dice	say
koarahɨ	sol	sun
dzasɨ	luna	moon
*dzasɨtatá (little known), estreya	estrella	star
ɨ	agua	water

* Spanish loan words

Guarani	Spanish	English
tatatį	humo	smoke
tatá	fuego	fire
tanimbú	ceniza	ashes
hendí	arde	burn
tapé	camino	road (path)
hagué	pluma	feather
áva, akarangué	cabello	hair
aká	cabeza	head
nambí	oreja	ear
hesá	ojo	eye
pi	pie	foot
renipiá, tipi?á	rodilla	knee
po	mano	hand
pi?á, hié	barriga	belly
adzúra	cuello	neck
oisu?ú	muerde	bite
oheshá	vee	see
ohendú	oye	hear
oikuaa	sabe	know
oké	duerme	sleep
oú	viene	come
oñenǫ	acuesta	lie
oguapí	sienta	sit
opu?á	levanta	stand
omę?ę́	da	give
amá	lluvia	rain
itá	piedra	stone
ivikuí	arena	sand
iví	tierra	earth
araí	nube	cloud
*sero	cerro	mountain
pitą́	rojo	red
hoví	verde	green
saidzú	amarillo	yellow
mǫrotį́	blanco	white

* Spanish loan words

Guarani	Spanish	English
hų	negro	black
pɨharé	noche	night
hakú	caliente	warm (hot)
roɨ́	frio	cold
henɨhé	lleno	full
pɨahú	nuevo	new
porą́, buéno	bueno	good
apuá	redondo	round
ką	seco	dry
héra	nombre	name

APPENDIX II: — INTERVIEW SCHEDULES

QUESTIONNAIRE ON LINGUISTIC USAGE

Nombre ....

Casa Número .... Lugar ....

Fecha .... Sexo .... Edad .... Donde Nació ....

Su conocimiento de Castellano ....

Ocupación ahora .... otro tiempo ....

Educación ....

Viajes ....

....

Responde a la pregunta con decir que lengua Usted usaría en caso caso—diciendo "Castellano" o "Guaraní"

1. Con su esposo diariamente ....
2. Con su esposo cuando está enojado ....
3. Con sus padres ....
4. Con su esposo en frente de las criaturas ....
5. Con su novia en la calle ....
6. Con su novia haciendo el amor ....
7. Con sus hijos ....
8. Con sus amigos tomando el terere (mate) ....
9. Con sus amigos en la calle ....
10. Con su marchante en el mercado ....
11. Con su patrón ....
12. Con su personal ....
13. Para hacer chistes ....
14. Con el médico ....
15. Con el curandero ....
16. Con una persona desconocida en vestido de traje ....
17. Con su sirvienta diariamente ....
18. Con sus abuelos ....
19. Con su madrina ....
20. Con el comisario u intendente ....

21. Con una señora en falda larga con sigarro poguasu
22. Para confesar
23. Con la madre de su novia u esposa
24. Con su sirvienta cuando está enojado
25. En un baile
26. Cuando está enojado
27. Con personas extrañas bien vestidas
28. Con la maestra de la escuela
29. Con las autoridades de Asunción
30. Con una señora vieja descalza
31. Con un desconocido
32. En la campaña
33. En la ciudad o pueblo
34. Con sus vecinos
35. Cuando está tomando caña (vino)
36. Con sus amigas (amigos) en las calles de Asunción
37. Con el guarda de un omnibus
38. Cuando quiere decir una cosa muy íntima
39. Con sus hermanos

APPENDIX II

HOUSEHOLD CENSUS SCHEDULE

COMPAÑIA .... CASA No. .... MANZANA No. .... LOTE No. ....

A. MIEMBROS DE LA FAMILIA

	Nombre	Edad	Sexo	Trabajo	Residencia	Estado Civil	Lugar de Nacimiento
PADRE							
MADRE							
hijos vivos y muertos 1							
2							
3							
4							
5							
6							
7							
8							
9							
10							
ABUELOS 1							
2							
3							
4							

B. OTRAS PERSONAS QUE VIVEN EN LA CASA

	Nombre	Edad	Sexo	Trabajo	Residencia	Estado Civil	Lugar de Nacimiento
1							
2							
3							
4							

C. DATOS SOBRE LA FAMILIA

1 Quién es el jefe:

2 Cuantos años están casados las parejas

    a) ....

    b) ....

3 Otras residencias que el actual y tiempo en cada uno

   a) Miembros de la familia

   b) Otras personas

D. LENGUA

1 Idioma de la casa
   a) Entre parejas: Español – Guarani – Ambos – Dzopará
   b) Con los niños: Español – Guarani – Ambos – Dzopará

2 Con que edad aprendió cada miembro el Español, dónde y de quien

	Edad	Donde	De quien
1			
2			
3			
4			
5			
6			
7			
8			
9			
10			
11			
12			

3 Historia de prohibición de guaraní (escuela, trabajo, etc.)

4 Opinión dónde se debe hablar
   Castellano:

   Guaraní:

E. COMUNICACIÓN

   Tiene radio: Si – No

  Lee: Diario: Si – No

     Acaé: Si – No

	HABLA	ESCRIBE	ENTIENDE	NOMBRE	GRADO
1. Español:	NO – M – B	NO – M – B	NO – M – B		
Guarani:	NO – M – B	NO – M – B	NO – M – B		
2. Español;	NO – M – B	NO – M – B	NO – M – B		
Guarani:	NO – M – B	NO – M – B	NO – M – B		
3. Español:	NO – M – B	NO – M – B	NO – M – B		
Guaraní:	NO – M – B	NO – M – B	NO – M – B		
4. Español:	NO – M – B	NO – M – B	NO – M – B		
Guaraní:	NO – M – B	NO – M – B	NO – M – B		
5. Español:	NO – M – B	NO – M – B	NO – M – B		
Guaraní:	NO – M – B	NO – M – B	NO – M – B		
6. Español:	NO – M – B	NO – M – B	NO – M – B		
Guaraní:	NO – M – B	NO – M – B	NO – M – B		
7. Español:	NO – M – B	NO – M – B	NO – M – B		
Guaraní:	NO – M – B	NO – M – B	NO – M – B		
8. Español:	NO – M – B	NO – M – B	NO – M – B		
Guarani:	NO – M – B	NO – M – B	NO – M – B		
9. Español:	NO – M – B	NO – M – B	NO – M – B		
Guaraní:	NO – M – B	NO – M – B	NO – M – B		
10. Español:	NO – M – B	NO – M – B	NO – M – B		
Guaraní:	NO – M – B	NO – M – B	NO – M – B		

Idioma de casa: Entre parejas: Español – Guaraní – ambos – yopará

               Entre los niños: Español – Guaraní – ambos – yopará

Razones por insistir en castellano ....

....

Opinión sobre el guaraní ....

....

BIBLIOGRAPHY

A. BOOKS AND ARTICLES

Azara, Felix de, *Descripción é Historia del Paraguay y del Rio de la Plata* (Buenos Aires, Impreso de los Talleres Gráficos, 1943). First Spanish edition in 1847.

Baez, Aida L. de Trigo, Louis A., and Gustavo A. Lezcano, *Lecciones de Castellano* (Asunción, El Indio, 1948).

Barker, George C., "Social Functions of Language in a Mexican-American Community", *Acta Americana*, V (1947), pp. 185-202.

——, , "Social Functions of Language in a Mexican-American Community", Unpublished doctoral dissertation, Department of Anthropology, University of Chicago, 1948.

Bertoni, Guillermo Tell, "La Lengua Guaraní", *Boletín del Instituto de Investigaciones*, Informes y Publicidad, Museo, Archivo y Biblioteca Bertoni, No. 2 (1936).

Bertoni, Moises Santiago, *Ortografía Guaraní Sobre la Base de la Ortografía Internacional Adoptada, por los Congresos de Zoología Botánica, con Arreglo á la Ortografía Lingüística Adoptada por el Congreso Científica Internacional de Buenos Aires (1910) y á la Generalmente Seguida por los Lingüistas Norteamericanos ...* (Asunción, M. Brossa, 1914).

Bottignoli, Justo, *Gramática Razonada de la Lengua Guaraní* (Montevideo, A. Monteverde and Cía, 1940).

Bianchetti, Juan, *Gramática Guaraní (Avañeé) y Principios de Filología; Ortografia Fonética, Analogía, Sintaxis, Construcción de Oraciones, Literatura (Prosa y Verso)* (Buenos Aires, Editorial Argentina Aristides Quillet, s.a., 1954).

Brown, Roger and Marguerite Ford, "Address in American English", *Journal of Abnormal and Social Psychology*, LXII (March, 1961), pp. 375-385.

Brown, Roger and Albert Gilman, "The Pronouns of Power and Solidarity", in Thomas A. Sebeok, ed., *Style in Language* (New York, The Technology Press of the Massachusetts Institute of Technology and John Wiley and Sons, 1960), pp. 253-276.

Buzó Gomes, Sinforiano, *Indice de la Poesía Paraguaya* (Asunción, Editorial Tupa, 1943).

Cáceres Zorilla, Cirilo, *Lecciones de Gramática Castellana por Cirilo Cáceres Zorilla....* (Villarica, El Guairá, 1939).

Cardogan, Leon, "En Torno al Bilingüismo en el Paraguay", *Revista de Antropología*, VI (1948), pp. 23-30.

Cardozo, Efraím, *Historiografía Paraguaya* (Mexico, Instituto Panamericano de Geografía e Historia — Comisión de Historia, 1959).

——, *Apuntes de Historia Cultural del Paraguay*, 2 vols. (Asunción, Colegio de San José, 1963).

——, *Breve historia del Paraguay* (Buenos Aires, Editorial Universitaria de Buenos Aires, 1965).

Casagrande, Joseph B., "Comanche Linguistic Acculturation", *International Journal of American Linguistics*, XX (1954), pp. 140-181, 217-237; XXI (1955), pp. 8-25.

Centurión, Carlos R., *Historia de las Letras Paraguayas*, 3 vols. (Buenos Aires, Editorial Ayachucho, 1947).

Centurión, Juan Crisóstomo, *Memorias del Coronel Juan Crisóstomo Centurión ó sea Reminisencias históricas sobre la guerra del Paraguay* (Buenos Aires, J. A. Berra, 1894).

Chamorro, Delfín, "La Enseñanza de la Gramática en Nuestros Colegios", *Revista del Centro de Estudiantes Normales*, II (1914).
Chapman, Charles Edward, *Colonial Hispanic America: A History* (New York, The MacMillan Company, 1933).
Chaves, Julio Cesar, *El Supremo Dictador* (Buenos Aires, Editorial Difusam, 1942).
Davenport, William, "The Family System of Jamaica", *Social and Economic Studies*, X (1961), pp. 420-454.
Decoud, Hector Francisco, *La Convención Nacional Constituyente y La Carta Magna de la República* (Buenos Aires, Talleres Gráficos Argentinos L. J. Rosso, 1934).
Decoud Larrosa, Reinaldo, "Ortografía Guaraní", *Revista del Ateneo Paraguayo Asunción*, Año 4, No. 16 (1946), pp. 17-19.
De Gaspari, Luís, *Laudatoria del Vernáculo La Poesía en Guaraní* (Buenos Aires, Continental, 1957).
Dominguez, Manuel, "Las Escuelas en el Paraguay" (Conference, Instituto Paraguayo de la Asunción, September 25, 1897).
——, *El Alma de la Raza* (Asunción, Casa Editora de Cándido Zamphiropolos, 1918).
——, ——, *El Alma de la Raza* (Buenos Aires, Editorial Ayacucho, 1946).
Diebold, A. Richard, "Incipient Bilingualism", *Language*, XXXVII (1961a), pp. 97-112.
——, "Bilingualism and Biculturalism in a Huave Community", Unpublished doctoral dissertation, Department of Anthropology, Yale University, 1961b.
——, "Mexican and Guatemalan Bilingualism", in Frank A. Rice, ed., *Study of the Role of Second Languages in Asia, Africa, and Latin America* (Washington, Center for Applied Linguistics, 1962), pp. 26-33.
——, "Code-Switching in Greek-English Bilingual Speech", in Elizabeth D. Woodworth, *et al.*, eds., *Proceedings of the Thirteenth Annual Round Table Meeting on Linguistics and Language Studies* (Spring 1962, Monograph Number 15) (Washington, Georgetown University Press, 1963), pp. 53-62.
Ervin-Tripp, Susan, "An Analysis of the Interaction of Language, Topic, and Listener", in John J. Gumperz and Dell Hymes, eds. *The Ethnography of Communication, American Anthropologist*, 66 (1964), pp. 86-102.
Febrés, Andrés, *Arte de Lengua General del Reyno de Chile; con un Diálogo Chileno-Hispano muy Curioso; a que se Añade la Doctrina Christiana, esto es, Rezo, Catecismo, Confesionario, y Pláticas; lo mas en Lengua Chilena y Castellana: y por fin un Vocabulario Hispano-Chileno, y un Calepino Chileno-Hispano mas Copioso* ([Santiago?], En la Calle de la Encarnación, 1765).
Ferguson, Charles A., "Diglossia", *Word* XV (1959a), pp. 325-340.
——, "Myths about Arabic", in *Proceedings of the Tenth Annual Round Table Meeting on Linguistics and Language Studies* (Washington, Georgetown University Press, 1959b), pp. 75-82.
——, and John Gumperz, eds. *Linguistic Diversity in South Asia: Studies in Regional, Social and Functional Variation*, Part III, *International Journal of American Linguistics*, XXVI (1960).
Fishman, Joshua, "Language Maintenance and Language Shift as a Field of Inquiry", *Linguistics*, 9 (1964), pp. 32-70.
Frake, Charles O., "The Diagnosis of Disease Among the Subanun of Mindanao", *American Anthropologist*, 63 (1961), pp. 113-32.
Friedrich, Paul, "Languages and Politics in India", *Daedalus*, XCI (1962), pp. 543-559.
——, "Structural Implications of Russian Pronominal Usage", forthcoming in: *Proceedings of the Los Angeles Conference in Sociolinguistics* (The Hague, Mouton and Company).
Gandía, Enrique de, *Franciso de Alfaro y la Condición Social de los Indios* (Buenos Aires, El Ateneo, 1939).
——, *Indios y Conquistadores en el Paraguay* (Buenos Aires, A Garcia Santos, 1932).
Gardner, Robert C. and W. E. Lambert, "Motivational Variables in Second-Language Acquisition", *Canadian Journal of Psychology*, XIII (1959), pp. 266-272.
Garvin, Paul L. and Madelaine Mathiot, "The Urbanization of the Guarani Language: A Problem in Language and Culture", in Anthony Wallace, ed., *Proceedings of the Fifth International Congress of Anthropological and Ethnological Sciences* (Philadelphia, University of Pennsylvania Press, 1960).
Gatti, Carlos D., *Vocabulario Guaraní-Español para Uso Médico* (Asunción, 1947).

Geertz, Clifford, "Linguistic Etiquette", in *The Religion of Java* (Glencoe, Illinois, The Free Press, 1960), pp. 248-260.

González, Antonio E., "Hispanismos en el Guaraní", *Boletín de Filología*, VI (1950), pp. 58-65.

——, and Tomas Osuna, *Diccionario Guaraní-Espãnol y Español-Guaraní*, 2nd edn. (Buenos Aires, Editorial Tupa, 1951).

Goodenough, Ward H., "Componential Analysis and the Study of Meaning", *Language*, XXXII (1956), pp. 195-212.

——, "Formal Properties of Status Relationships", Unpublished paper read before the 1961 Meetings of the American Anthropological Association.

Guasch, Antonio, *El Idioma Guaraní; Gramática y Antología de Prosa y Verso*, 3rd edn. (Asunción, Casa América-Moreno Hnos., 1956).

Guttman, Louis, "The Basis for Scalogram Analysis", in *Studies in Social Psychology in World War II*, vol. 4, pp. 60-90 (Princeton, Princeton University Press, 1950).

Harrison, Selig S., *The Most Dangerous Decades* (New York, Language and Communication Research Center of Columbia University, 1957).

Haugen, Einar I., *The Norwegian Language in America: a Study in Bilingual Behavior*, 2 vols. (Philadelphia, University of Pennsylvania Press, 1953).

——, *Bilingualism in the Americas: A Bibliography and Research Guide* (University, Alabama, The American Dialect Society, 1956).

Hasselmo, Nils, "American Swedish: A Study in Bilingualism", Unpublished doctoral dissertation, Department of Linguistics, Harvard University, 1961.

Hyppolite, Michelson Paul, *Le Devenir du Créole Haitien; Conference Prononcée au Pavillion des Beaux-Arts, le 7 Août 1952* (Port-au-Prince, Imprimerie de l'Etat, 1952).

Jover Peralta, Anselmo, *El Guaraní en la Geografía de América. Diccionario de Guaranismos* (Buenos Aires, Editorial Tupa, Artes Gráficas de Vinne, 1950).

Lambert, Wallace E., "Measurement of the Linguistic Dominance of Bilinguals", *Journal of Abnormal and Social Psychology*, L (1955), pp. 197-200.

Leyburn, James G., *The Haitian People* (New Haven, Yale University Press, 1941).

Lounsbury, Floyd G., "A Semantic Analysis of the Pawnee Kinship Usage", *Language*, XXXII (1956), pp. 158-194.

Lezcano, Luís, *Actualidad de Andrés Bello y Delfín Chamorro* (Asunción, La Colmena, s. a., 1946).

Morínigo, Marcos A., *Hispanismos en el Guaraní* (Buenos Aires, Instituto de Filología Colección de Estudios Indigenistas, 1931).

——, "Influencia del Español en la Estructura Lingüística del Guaraní", *Filología*, Año V (1959), pp. 235-248.

Nader, Laura, "A Note on Attitudes and the Use of Language", *Anthropological Linguistics*, IV (1962), pp. 24-29.

Nociones Elementales de Catecismo en Lengua Guaraní (Asunción, 1910).

Ortiz Mayans, Antonio, *Diccionario Guaraní-castellano, Castellano-guaraní; con un compendio gramatical*, 6th edn. (Buenos Aires, 1949).

Peramás, José Manuel, *La República de Platón y los Guaraníes* (Buenos Aires, Emecé, Editores, s.a., 1946). 1st edition, 1791.

Raphael, Maxwell and Jerimiah Ford, *A Tentative Bibliography of Paraguayan Literature* (Cambridge, Harvard University Press, 1934).

Reh, Emma, *Paraguayan Rural Life* (Washington, Institute of Inter-American Affairs, Food Supply Division, 1946).

Restivo, Paulo R., *Linguae Guarani Grammatica ... a Rev. P. Iesuita Paulo Restivo Secundum Libros Antonio Ruiz de Montoya, Simonis Bandini Aliorumque, Adieto Particularum Lexico, Anno MDCCXXIV in Ciuitate Sanctae Mariae Maioris Edita* (Stuttgart, 1892).

——, *Vocabulario de la Lengua Guaraní, Comp. por el P. A. Ruiz de Montoya, Revisto y Aumentado por el P. Paulo Restivo* (Pueblo de Sta. María la Mayor, 1722).

Rice, Frank A., ed., *Study of the Role of Second Languages in Asia, Africa, and Latin America* (Washington, Center for Applied Linguistics, 1962).

Robertson, John P., *La Argentina en la Época de la Revolución. Cartas sobre el Paraguay: Comprendiendo la Relación de Una Residencia de Cuatro Años en esa República, Bajo el Gobierno del Dictador Francia* (Buenos Aires, Administración General Vaccaro, 1920).

Rodriguéz, Mariano C., *Gramática de la Lengua Quechua*, 3rd. edn. (Lima, Editorial Librería Peruana, 1939).

Rojas y Villaseca, Mariano Jacobo, *Estudios Gramaticales del Idioma Mexicano* (Mexico City, Impr. de J. D. Rojas, 1935).

Rowe, John H., "The Distribution of Indians and Indian Languages in Peru", *Geographical Review*, XXXVII (1947), pp. 202-215.

Rubin, Joan, "Bilingualism in Paraguay", *Anthropological Linguistics*, IV (1962), pp. 52-58.

——, "The Use of Componential Analysis in Culture Change", Unpublished paper read before the 1965 Meetings of the American Anthropological Association.

Rubio, Julián María, *Exploración y Conquista del Río de la Plata: Siglos XVI y XVII* (Buenos Aires, Salvat Editores, 1942).

Ruiz de Montoya, Antonio, *Arte de la Lengua Guaraní*, 2 vols. (Leipzig, B. G. Teubner, 1876).

——, *Tesoro de la Lengua Guaraní* (Leipzig, B. G. Teubner, 1876).

Salas, Alberto Mario, "El Paraíso de Mahoma Crónica del Mestizaje en el Río de la Plata", *Revista de la Universidad de Buenos Aires*, V Epoca, Año II (1958), pp. 521-542.

Samuel, Maurice, *Harvest in the Desert* (Philadelphia, The Jewish Publication Society of America, 1944).

Schaedel, R. P., *el al.*, *Plan Regional Para El Desarrollo del Sur*, Vol. XXVII: Los Recursos de la Region: Recomendaciones para su Desarrollo (Lima, 1959).

Service, Elman R., *Spanish-Guarani Relations in Early Colonial Paraguay*, No. 9: Anthropological Papers of the Museum of Anthropology, University of Michigan (Ann Arbor, University of Michigan Press, 1954a).

——, and Helen S. Service, *Tobatí: Paraguayan Town* (Chicago, The University of Chicago Press, 1954b).

Steward, Julian H. and Louis C. Faron, *Native Peoples of South America* (New York, McGraw Hill, 1959).

Stewart, Wm. A., "Creole Languages in the Caribbean", in Frank A. Rice, ed., *Study of the Role of Second Languages in Asia, Africa, and Latin America* (Washington, Center for Applied Linguistics, 1962), pp. 34-53.

Suarez, Emma G. and Jorge Alberto, "A Description of Colloquial Guarani", Unpublished doctoral dissertation, Department of Linguistics, Cornell University, 1961.

Swadesh, Morris, "Sociological Notes on Obsolescent Languages", *International Journal of American Linguistics*, XIV (1948), pp. 226-235.

Urioste, Jorge, *Gramática de la Lengua Quechua y Vocabulario Quechua-castellano, Castellano-quechua de las Voces más Usuales* (La Paz, Editorial Canata, 1955).

Valdovinos, Arnaldo, *La Incógnita del Paraguay* (Buenos Aires, Editorial Atlantida, s.a., 1945).

Velazquez, Rafael Eladio, "Paraguay", *Anuario de Estudios Americanos*, XV (1958), pp. 675-686.

Warren, Harris Gaylord, *Paraguay, an Informal History* (Norman, Univ. of Oklahoma Press, 1949).

Washburn, Charles A., *The History of Paraguay*, 2 vols. (Boston, Lee and Shepard, 1871).

Weinreich, Uriel, "Research Problems in Bilingualism with Special Reference to Switzerland", Unpublished doctoral dissertation, Department of Linguistics, Columbia University, 1951.

——, *Languages in Contact, Findings and Problems* (New York, Linguistic Circle of New York, 1953).

Wey, Walter, *La Poesía Paraguaya: Historia de Una Incógnita* (Montevideo, Biblioteca Alfor, 1951).

Windmiller, Marshall, "Linguistic Regionalism in India", *Pacific Affairs*, XXVII (1954), pp. 291-318.

B. DOCUMENTS, PERIODICALS AND NEWSPAPERS

ACA'É, Asunción, Paraguay. 1957-1961.

"Acta de la Fundación de la Academía de la Lengua y Cultura Guaraní: Postulados y Declaración de Principios" (Asunción, 1942). (Mimeographed).

"Alfabeto Fonético Para Las Lenguas Quechua y Aymara", in *Actas Finales de los Tres Primeros Congresos Indigenistas Inter-americanos* (Guatemala City, Editorial del Ministerio de Educación Pública, 1959).

Analfabetismo y Nivel de Educación, Vol. IV: La Estructura Demográfica de las Naciones Americanas: Análisis Estadístico-censal de los Resultados Obtenidos Bajo el Programa del Censo de las Américas de 1950 (COTA—1950) (Washington, Unión Panamericana, 1960).

Anuario Estadístico de la República del Paraguay 1948-1953 (Asunción, Ministerio de Hacienda Dirección General de Estadística y Censos, 1955).

Carroll, John B. and Wai-Cheng Ho, "Pictorial Auditory Comprehension Test" (New York, Modern Language Association, 1959).

Censo Nacional de Población y Ocupación 1940 (Lima, 1942).

de Riberas, Lázaro, Unpublished "Informe del Gobernador del Paraguay, Lázaro de Riberas, al Rey de España" (Asunción, December 22, 1797).

"Escritura de las Lenguas Quechua y Aymara. Tres Documentos Sobre el Sistema de Escritura de Estas Lenguas Aprobado y Recomendado por el III Congreso Indigenista Interamericano de La Paz, Bolivia, 1954", *Ciencias y Arte* (Cuzco, Peru, 1954).

Fernando de Pinedo, Agustín, Unpublished "Informe del Gobernador del Paraguay, Agustín Fernando de Pinedo, al Rey de España Sobre la Provincia del Paraguay" (Asunción, January 29, 1777). [Published in: Revista del Instituto Paraguayo, 52 (1905)].

Greenberg, Joseph, "The Study of Language Contact in Africa", paper read at the Second Meeting of the Inter-African Committee on Linguistics, Symposium on Multilingualism (Brazzaville, July, 1962) (Mimeographed).

Guggiari, Bruno, Personal Letter to Julio Correa, 1933.

Instrucciones para los maestros de Escuelas por la Junta Superior Gubernativa (Asunción, February 15, 1812).

Lewis, E. Glyn, "Conditions Affecting the 'Reception' of an 'Official' (Second/Foreign Language)", paper read at the Second Meeting of the Inter-African Committee on Linguistics, Symposium on Multilingualism (Brazzaville, July, 1962) (Mimeographed).

"Ortografía de la Lengua Guaraní" (Asunción, Imprenta Nacional, 1940).

Primer Congreso de la Lengua Tupi-Guaraní de Montevideo, "Proceedings", in *Boletín de Filología* [Montevideo , V (1949), and VI (1950), *passim.*

Revista del Ateneo Paraguayo (Asunción, 1940-1961).

Revista de Turismo (Asunción, 1942-1944).

Segundo Congreso Internacional de la Lengua y Cultura Guaraní-Tupí, "Resoluciones y Recomendaciones", in *Boletín de Filología* [Montevideo], VII (1953), pp. 679-685.

Séptimo Censo General de Población, 6 de junio de 1950: Resumen (Mexico City, Dirección General de Estadística, 1953).

[text illegible]